ENDORSEMENTS

style draws us in, her humor and honesty keep us turning the pages with anticipation, and the faith lessons she shares stay with us."
—**Susan B. Wilson,** MBA, CSP, Executive Strategies

"I so enjoyed *How Can I Run a Tight Ship When I'm Surrounded by Loose Cannons?* In fact, I enjoyed it so much that allowing myself to read a chapter became my 'reward' for getting things done. I felt like I really got to know Kathi through her journey to become a Proverbs 31 woman, and I related to each and every one of her hiccups along the way! (About the time I think I've got things figured out, a loose cannon always rolls through my life too!) I just love how God uses unlikely people and circumstances to mold us into who and what He wants us to be."
—**Deanne R. Herr,** Executive Strategies

"Let Kathi help you sail through your life's uncharted waters with her delightful book, *How Can I Run a Tight Ship When I'm Surrounded by Loose Cannons?* Chuckle as Kathi tells how she's not only dodged loose cannonballs, but learned how to trust God through the process. So don't abandon ship, you're in for an adventure that will splash your life with joy."
—**Linda Evans Shepherd,** coauthor of "The Potluck Club" Series

"This laugh-out-loud book is ideal for today's work-in-progress women. It's a delightful blend of humor, Scripture, and insight that keeps you turning the pages. True to Kathi's spiritual maturity, she keeps the life-ship telescope pointed toward our great Captain."
—**Jan Coates,** author/speaker/consultant, founder and president of Set Free Today ministries

"Through humor and vulnerability, Kathi Macias paints a picture to which every woman who thinks 'perfect' is a destination can relate. *How Can I Run a Tight Ship When I'm Surrounded by Loose Cannons?* is a refreshing reminder that God has the cannons and our proverbial ships in His hands."

—**Stacy Hawkins Adams,** author of *Watercolored Pearls, Nothing but the Right Thing,* and *Speak to My Heart*

"With her characteristic warmth, candor, and a wealth of zany humor, Kathi Macias helps readers see beyond the myth of the Proverbs 31 woman."

—**Kacy Barnett-Gramckow,** author of "The Genesis Trilogy," Moody Publishers

HOW CAN I RUN A
TIGHT SHIP
WHEN I'M SURROUNDED BY
LOOSE CANNONS?

PROVERBS 31 DISCOVERIES FOR
YIELDING TO THE MASTER OF THE SEAS

KATHI MACIAS

NEW HOPE
PUBLISHERS
Birmingham, Alabama

New Hope® Publishers
P. O. Box 12065
Birmingham, AL 35202-2065
www.newhopepublishers.com

New Hope Publishers is a division of WMU®.

Library of Congress Cataloging-in-Publication Data

Mills-Macias, Kathi, 1948-
  How can I run a tight ship when I'm surrounded by loose cannons? : Proverbs 31 discoveries for yielding to the master of the seas / Kathi Macias.
    p. cm.
  ISBN-13: 978-1-59669-204-6 (sc)
  ISBN-10: 1-59669-204-9 (sc)
  1. Bible. O.T. Proverbs XXXI, 10-31--Criticism, interpretation, etc.
  I. Title.
  BS1465.52.M56 2009
  242'.5--dc22
                        2008041409

ISBN-10: 1-59669-204-9
ISBN-13: 978-1-59669-204-6

N084127 0209 3M1

Dedication

To all those gracious people* God has placed in my life through the years to model for me the realities of the Proverbs 31 woman, even as I rushed around in my quest to defuse the loose cannons in my life;

To my dear husband and best friend, Al, who loves me even when I'm the exact opposite of the Proverbs 31 woman and who has protected me from a lot of loose cannons that seemed determined to mow me down;

And to the One who has promised to complete the good work He has started in me, which is my only hope for ever becoming a Proverbs 31 woman…
Thank you!

*All stories contained in this book are based on true events, though some of the names/details have been changed—not so much to protect the innocent but to compensate for the author's advancing age and regressing memory. The principle in each story is true, however, so read and enjoy…and have a laugh or two along the way.

TABLE OF CONTENTS

Foreword by Martha Bolton: Red Lips and Fat Hair 11

Introduction: Will the Real Superwoman Please Stand Up? 15

Section One:
Learning to Crawl—On My Knees 19
Chapter 1   Reality Check 23
Chapter 2   Strike Two 29
Chapter 3   Food Court Fiasco 35
Chapter 4   The Woman with 97 Children 41
Chapter 5   A Shot at Redemption 49

Section Two:
Learning to Walk—Slow and Shaky, but on My Feet 55
Chapter 6   Gotcha! 59
Chapter 7   Face-Plants 65
Chapter 8   "Who Signed Me Up for That?" 73
Chapter 9   What an Embarrassment 79
Chapter 10   My Machete-Wielding Family 85

Section Three:
Learning to Run—Swift and Steady, Still on My Feet 91
Chapter 11   You Mean It's Not About Me? 95
Chapter 12   Imogene's Dolls 103
Chapter 13   "When Were You Going to Tell Me?" 109
Chapter 14   Locusts and Wild Honey, Anyone? 115
Chapter 15   "Don't Forget to Write" 121

Section Four:
Learning to Fly—Soaring with Eagles 127
Chapter 16   A Change in Flight Plans 131
Chapter 17   Getting to the Root of Fear 137
Chapter 18   A Child Will Lead Them 143
Chapter 19   "Who's *She*?" 149
Chapter 20   Cell Groups 155

Section Five:
Learning to Lean—Back on My Knees 161
Chapter 21   Gone Off the Deep End 165
Chapter 22   Back Home Again 173
Chapter 23   Bernadine Returns 181
Chapter 24   "Somebody Has to Set up the Chairs" 187
Chapter 25   "Under the Mercy" 193

Conclusion: O Captain, My Captain 201

Afterword by Rhonda Rhea:
Coffee, Chocolate, and Smoking Bangs 203

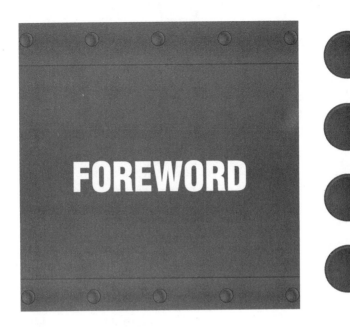

FOREWORD

Red Lips and Fat Hair

I met Kathi Macias in a writers' group about 20 years ago, and we've been friends ever since. In fact, it wasn't long after we met that we both started publishing books and realized we needed to have professional photographs taken for publicity. When Kathi ran across an ad in the paper—one of those two-for-one coupon types—promoting a studio that offered to do our hair and make-up, and even provide glamorous clothing, it sounded too good to be true. But we decided to go for it.

I suppose that's where we really bonded, as we sat next to each other watching our transformation in the mirror. The makeup part was fun, since I usually go pretty much "as is," and this was very much a new experience for me. But as they began applying the third or fourth layer, I asked myself, *Does this look professional?* I didn't say anything, though, because I certainly didn't want to complain.

I now know that I probably should have said something as the makeup artist started penciling in new lips for me. After all, she only had so much room to work with because my nose was in the way. But it seemed like she was taking every centimeter of facial real estate and claiming it in the name of my lips. By the time she was done, you could have spotted my lips from the other end of the state. And I don't think I had ever seen that bright a shade of red before. But still, I didn't want to complain....

Next came my hair. Now, I have fine, thin hair, so when the stylist asked if I wanted her to add more volume, I readily agreed. The next thing I knew she had teased and ratted my fine, thin hair until it stood so high that eagles would have gotten nosebleeds trying to nest there. My hair was bigger than Texas, and she was still going. The bigger my hair got, the more I thought about speaking up—after all, this picture was for future book covers—but as I said, I didn't want to complain.

Then it was time to choose an outfit. No one had warned me that if I wanted to wear something that wouldn't get me arrested, I would have to bring it from home. But I was stuck, so I picked a shiny top, threw on a couple of feathery boas, and I was ready. (The picture has yet to make the cover of a book, but my husband liked it, and I guess that's what really matters in the long run, so I'm glad I didn't complain.)

At last, there I was, in all my big-hair and glitzy clothes and makeup, wondering just what kind of books they thought I wrote. And then I saw Kathi—at least, I was pretty sure that's who it was—and I remembered she had been going through the same ordeal. I can't really explain it, but for some strange reason, seeing her with her own fat hair and sequined outfit made me feel a little better.

By the time we finally got out of that place (back in our own clothes...but still sporting fat hair and painted faces), we were starved but afraid to go into a restaurant for fear of being arrested. So we opted for a drive-through. When the lady at the window handed us our burgers, her eyes were nearly as big as our bright red lips!

I can't tell you how many laughs we had that day, but it has turned out to be one of my funniest and fondest memories.

Since then, Kathi has gone on to write so many books that I've lost count, and chances are she's had some new photographs done as well—minus the boas, of course. So when I was asked to write a foreword for her book about loose cannons, I somehow felt that in light of our past experience it would be appropriate to do so.

Now I'm sure most of us have at least one "loose cannon" in our lives—and probably many of us qualify as loose cannons ourselves. So if you find yourself becoming frustrated as you try harder and harder to run a tight ship, but all you end up doing is dodging loose cannons on your ever-rolling deck, this is the book that will help you get your sea legs. With humor and plenty of good advice, Kathi will help you learn to listen to your Captain—and make your way into peaceful waters.

And if you ever want a glamour picture taken, I'm sure Kathi can help you arrange that, too. (But feel free to complain—please!)

—**Martha Bolton**, Emmy-nominated songwriter and author of *Didn't My Skin Used to Fit* and *Cooking With Hot Flashes*

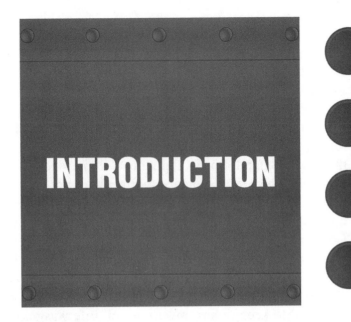

INTRODUCTION

Will the Real Superwoman Please Stand Up?

I've always been a control freak who wanted everything to run smoothly—perfectly, actually. No bumps or surprises, just a "tight ship" as they say. And somewhere along the line I got the idea that I could make that happen—if I just tried hard enough. I think it may have started when I first saw *Adventures of Superman* on our family's black and white TV and wondered, *Is there a Superwoman somewhere?* When I put that question to the adults in my life, they smiled and patted me on the head and said, "I don't think so, dear." So I decided to sign up for the job—a reasonable if somewhat naïve aspiration for a 6-year-old, not so reasonable and way beyond naive at 26. Two decades after the birth of my superwoman dream, I was still running as fast as I could and getting nowhere. My 20-year-old dream was going down for the count, and I was nearly at the point of throwing in the towel. That's when I met Jesus.

What a difference! Now I could latch on to verses like *"I can do all things through Christ who strengthens me"* and *"Let all things be done decently and in order"*—biblical affirmations of my desire to do things right, to do things efficiently and effectively, and to do things with power and authority (Philippians 4:13; 1 Corinthians 14:40). I was invincible—in Jesus, of course.

And as I earnestly searched the Scriptures—eureka!—I found what I thought sounded like a biblical basis for my thinking: Proverbs 31. There, at last, was the epitome of the superwoman I'd been hoping to become since I was six years old. The perfect woman—perfect wife, perfect mother, perfect housekeeper, perfect entrepreneur—all rolled into one! Not only did her husband and children praise her, but God must have approved of her as well or He certainly wouldn't have included her as an example in the Bible. My superwoman dream was alive and well! At last I would be able to get it all together, to win instead of fail, to run a tight ship, and to keep things under control. Life was good, and the future looked bright.

There was only one problem. I hadn't figured on all the loose cannons rolling around the deck of my not-so-tight ship....

Proverbs 31:10–31 (NIV)

A wife of noble character who can find?
She is worth far more than rubies.
Her husband has full confidence in her and lacks nothing of value.
She brings him good, not harm, all the days of her life.
She selects wool and flax and works with eager hands.
She is like the merchant ships, bringing her food from afar.
She gets up while it is still dark; she provides food for her family and portions for her servant girls.
She considers a field and buys it; out of her earnings she plants a vineyard.
She sets about her work vigorously; her arms are strong for her tasks.
She sees that her trading is profitable, and her lamp does not go out at night.
In her hand she holds the distaff and grasps the spindle with her fingers.
She opens her arms to the poor and extends her hands to the needy.
When it snows, she has no fear for her household; for all of them are clothed in scarlet.
She makes coverings for her bed; she is clothed in fine linen and purple.
Her husband is respected at the city gate, where he takes his seat among the elders of the land.
She makes linen garments and sells them, and supplies the merchants with sashes.
She is clothed with strength and dignity; she can laugh at the days to come.
She speaks with wisdom, and faithful instruction is on her tongue.
She watches over the affairs of her household and does not eat the bread of idleness.
Her children arise and call her blessed; her husband also, and he praises her: "Many women do noble things, but you surpass them all."
Charm is deceptive, and beauty is fleeting; but a woman who fears the LORD is to be praised.
Give her the reward she has earned, and let her works bring her praise at the city gate.

LEARNING TO CRAWL— ON MY KNEES

Brothers, I could not address you as spiritual but as worldly— mere infants in Christ. I gave you milk, not solid food, for you were not yet ready for it. Indeed, you are still not ready.
—1 Corinthians 3:1–2 (NIV)

Rug Rats...and Other Myths

I'll never forget the time I spent a week with my son Michael and his family. One evening my granddaughter Karissa invited me to camp out on the sofa bed with her and watch a *Rugrats* movie while we ate microwave popcorn. Doting grandmother that I am, I immediately accepted, though I couldn't imagine what a *Rugrats* movie might be.

I'd heard the term, but never in relation to a movie. As far as I was concerned, rug rats were very small children, not yet able to walk but slightly too old to be considered infants. These tiny people crawled around the house on their hands and knees, scooted across the floor on their behinds, or inched their way from one spot to another in an ingenious imitation of an undulating caterpillar, all the while on the hunt for bugs, buttons, spare change, or anything else they could pop into their drooling mouths. Their world consisted of coffee table legs, the dog dish when Mom wasn't looking, grown-ups' feet, and... well, rugs. Was I now supposed to believe that Hollywood had literally sunk so low as to film an entire movie at floor level?

Popcorn bowl between us, my granddaughter and I settled back against our pillows and watched the opening minutes of her current favorite video. As the animated scenes rolled by, it didn't take long for me to admit that the cartoon kids were actually kind of cute, though a bit older than what I considered rug-rat age and definitely more adventurous than I wanted my own kids or grandkids to be—at any age. Overall, however, it was an enjoyable evening, and I'd been educated about the latest kiddie craze in movies.

That night brought back memories of more than two decades before, when I was in my mid-twenties and smack-dab in the middle of the raising rug rats stage of life myself. It was at that time I had the most incredible experience anyone can ever have: I became a Christian—a baby Christian, with a whole lot to learn. And as I said in the introduction, once I became a Christian I assumed my life would fall into perfect order. I would never again have so much as a bad-hair day. I set out to emulate the shipshape Proverbs 31 woman in every way possible. OK, so maybe I was the only human being on the face of the planet who didn't realize I had picked one of the worst possible times to decide to try to run a tight ship, but you have to give me an A for enthusiasm. I was quickly reminded, however, that there is another equally appropriate term for rug rats: *loose cannons*. And there's nothing like a bunch of loose cannons to wreak havoc on an otherwise tight ship. True, rug rats are relatively small cannons, but that doesn't make them any less deadly. Talk to any mother who's wearing herself out trying to keep her ship afloat while dodging those little cannons rolling around her feet and she'll tell you that *Mutiny on the Bounty* has become her life's theme. However, I wasn't content simply to keep my ship afloat; I was determined to run a tight ship just like the one navigated so expertly by the Proverbs 31 superwoman. Even she had to contend with rug rats at some point in her life, right? And nothing sank her ship! She sailed blissfully along, her sparkling clean and perfectly equipped vessel cutting smoothly through the water, as she enjoyed the praises of her family and the favor of God. Now that same God was on my side. What did I have to worry about?

Far too naive and immature to realize I was scarcely more than a spiritual rug rat myself, I decided I needed to pray more in order to achieve my goals—or fast more, or memorize more Scripture, or get more involved in Bible studies and women's ministries. Maybe I could learn something from talking to some of the "been there, done that" women at church, who now had their ships under control. Maybe they'd have some suggestions on how better to organize my time or plan my activities. Didn't the Bible say something about the older, more experienced women teaching the younger ones?

I now had the perfect plan, and I set out to implement it. All I had to do was pin down those successful women at church whose lives and families were already shipshape, and then put into practice everything I learned from their examples....

REALITY CHECK

Her laughter still rings in my ears decades later. I thought I'd chosen the godliest, most time-tested, got-it-all-together, mature woman in our church. But when I asked if she would teach me how to run a perfect household in line with that of the Proverbs 31 woman, Betty doubled over and laughed until tears rolled down her cheeks. I stood there, baffled, waiting for her to catch her breath. After ten minutes I nearly gave up and moved on to someone else, deciding Betty wasn't nearly as perfect as she had appeared. But when I started to back away, she laid her hand on my arm and motioned for me to stay.

"I'm sorry," she gasped, taking several deep breaths and trying to regain her composure. "I didn't mean to... It's just that..." Betty laughed again and shook her head as she wiped the tears from her eyes. A few more minutes of waiting on my part and Betty finally began to resemble the intelligent, reasonable woman I was used to seeing every Sunday morning. I breathed a sigh of relief.

"Truly," she said, "I didn't mean to laugh. But when you used the words 'perfect household' in reference to me and my family..." She shook her head again and sighed. "Forgive me. I'm not taking your request lightly. The Bible does say the older women are to teach the younger, and I'd be more than happy to help you. But if it's perfection you're looking for..." She paused and smiled. "I'm afraid Jesus is the only One who qualifies."

I returned her smile. I was a new Christian, but I certainly understood that no one was perfect except Jesus. Still, if His Spirit lives inside us, shouldn't being perfect be our goal?

I asked Betty that very question, and she nodded. "Right again. The Bible says we are to be perfect, just as God is perfect. However—"

Bingo! I didn't have time to hear about her "however." I was too caught up in the excitement of discovering another scripture to add to my repertoire of favorites—all of which supported my goal of running a tight ship. It looked like Betty might be able to help me after all.

Then she told me what seemed to be a completely unrelated story. It wasn't until much later that I understood how it all tied in to what God was teaching me about rug rats and crawling.

"It was during the Korean War," she began, guiding me over to a couple of empty chairs, where we settled in as she talked. "My husband, Charles, was serving overseas as an Army chaplain. Our boys were just little guys then—Charlie was almost two, and Danny was ten months. The boys and I lived in a tiny apartment not far from my parents' house, and one day my mom convinced me I needed to get out more. Believe me, with two kids in diapers, that was no easy assignment. But she insisted, even offering to watch the boys so I could visit with friends once in awhile.

"The more I thought about it, the more I thought she might be right. With Charles gone, I rarely saw anyone besides my parents and kids. I liked the idea of having someone my own age to talk to, so I called Eileen, one of my friends I hadn't seen since before Danny was born, and we made a date to meet for lunch the next day. By the time I got the boys and all their belongings over to Mom's house, I couldn't wait to get going.

"Charlie and Danny were excited too. They loved visiting with Grandma. As soon as we got there, my mom took them into the kitchen for peanut butter sandwiches and brownies. They scarcely noticed when I blew them kisses and said goodbye. I made a quick detour into the bathroom and then headed for the front door. I was just stepping out onto the porch when Charlie came running up behind me. He tugged at me and said something, but I didn't really catch what it was. I bent down and gave him one last kiss, then sent him back to Grandma."

Betty smiled again, her brown eyes twinkling. A bit of nostalgia, I supposed. And why not? She'd done everything right. The kids were safe and sound and having a great time with their grandmother; Betty's friend was undoubtedly on her way to the restaurant; everything had been done "decently and in order," just as prescribed in the Bible. Was that her point in telling me this story?

"You must have had a very nice time visiting with your friend," I commented, eager for her to get to the point.

Betty grinned. For a moment I was afraid she would erupt into laughter once again, but then she continued. "Yes, I did...eventually. But it took me a while to find her."

Now I was confused. How hard could it be to find a friend at a restaurant?

A Little Off?

"It was a beautiful spring day," Betty said. "The sun was shining, I was wearing my favorite pink dress and matching pumps, and I was on my way to have lunch with a dear friend. I can't tell you how much I enjoyed the half-mile walk to the little downtown café where Eileen and I used to go for ice cream when we were kids. I got there a few minutes early, so when I didn't see Eileen anywhere inside, I decided to wait for her out front. Nearly 30 minutes later I was still pacing back and forth in front of the café, wondering why so many people stared and grinned at me as they passed by. But most of all, I wondered where Eileen was! I have to admit, I was getting a little bit annoyed. I didn't get out very often, and I didn't want to spend the day waiting in front of the café while people strolled by, gawking and giggling. You'd think they'd never seen anyone pacing the sidewalk before. Besides, it wasn't like Eileen to be late."

Betty shook her head and sighed. "I checked my watch and went over everything in my mind. It was almost twelve thirty on Tuesday, and I knew we'd agreed on Tuesday at noon, right there at the café.... That's when I remembered. Eileen said she hadn't seen my mom in a long time and would love to say hello, plus she wanted to see my boys, so she was going to meet me at my mom's and then we'd walk to the restaurant together."

I didn't want to be rude, but I couldn't imagine how Betty could forget something so simple as where to meet her friend. Was it possible she was telling me this story to give me an example of how disorganized she once was, and then contrast it by explaining how she changed and became like the Proverbs 31 woman?

"Needless to say, I felt pretty ridiculous," Betty confessed. "I hurried back toward my mom's house, and halfway there I ran into Eileen, who'd given up waiting for me. We headed back to the café together and laughed all the way through lunch and had the greatest visit. She couldn't say enough about how adorable my boys were, and how good it was to see my mom."

Betty's eyes twinkled again. "When we finished lunch, I started out the door ahead of Eileen, and all of a sudden she burst out laughing. I turned to see what was so funny and noticed a few other people in the café looking my way, giggling and snickering. Then Eileen leaned over and whispered, 'Did you happen to notice a draft when you were walking?' I couldn't imagine what she was talking about, and then she said, 'Come on. Let's stop in the ladies' room for a minute.' I still didn't know what was going on, but my cheeks were flaming as we walked through the crowded eatery to the restroom in back. That's when I found out that my skirt was hiked up in the back, and I realized I must have caught it in the elastic waistband of my slip when I stopped in the bathroom just before I left my mom's house. Thank goodness I was wearing that slip!"

I was horrified, but the story wasn't over yet. Betty was laughing again, and I decided it was either insanity or the passing of time that enabled her to do so. Personally, I wasn't sure I'd ever recover had I been in her shoes. I smiled expectantly and waited for her to tell me how she learned from her experience and became more organized and "together" as a result. Instead she told me how she had discovered a small brown handprint—closer inspection revealed it was a brownie stain—on the back of her slip, five tiny fingers engraved in chocolate on white silk. It was then Betty realized what Charlie was trying to tell her when he tugged at her as she was leaving her mom's house.

She also told me how that embarrassing event had become one of her fondest memories, and how to this day she and Eileen still call one another on the phone to laugh about it. I could see how Eileen might find that particular memory amusing, but Betty? Like I said, only the passing of time—or just plain insanity—could account for that. I was leaning toward the latter.

What really confused me was why she didn't go on with her story and tell me all she'd learned from her humiliating experience—how to plan better, keep notes of details, check appearances before venturing out into public, make sure her children's hands were washed before they touched her. I could see some redeeming value in such a story if it had been the catalyst to launch her into a new and improved lifestyle. But she just smiled and told me she hoped I'd have such wonderful memories of my own some day. Then she prayed with me and asked God to bless this "very special time" in my life and to guide me into becoming the mature Christian woman He had designed me to be. She also offered to meet with me again sometime and told me to feel free to call her.

I appreciated her prayer and her offer, but decided maybe I had misread Betty when I classified her as someone who could help me become like the Proverbs 31 woman. She was a nice lady, but I now saw that her ship was listing badly to one side. If I was serious about achieving my goal of running my own tight ship, I would have to find a more reliable and balanced mentor.

Making It Personal

Consider times in your life when false expectations hindered you from enjoying or appreciating your circumstances. How can a more realistic or mature understanding of God's seasons for your life prevent you from missing out on what He has for you today?

To everything there is a season, a time for every purpose under heaven.
—Ecclesiastes 3:1

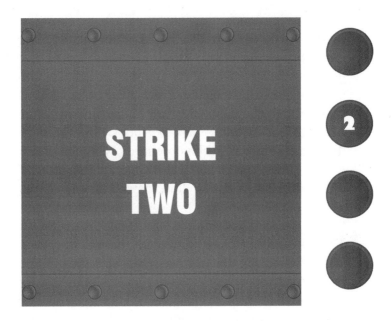

STRIKE TWO

2

OK, I was back to square one in my search for a role model. I realized I would have to be more discriminating in choosing a potential mentor. I thought through some possibilities. The senior pastor's wife was an obvious choice but far too busy. The youth pastor's wife wasn't much older than I was, so she was out. Judy, the choir director, was about the right age, but she'd never been married or had any kids, so I didn't see how she could help. I even considered one of my mother's friends, but... well, she was my mother's friend.

I was beginning to get discouraged when I remembered Ruth. I knew Ruth was getting up there in years—nearly 60, which at the time I considered fast approaching ancient—but the last I heard she was still mentally alert and physically healthy. I didn't see any reason to think it would take long to learn what I needed to know about being a Proverbs 31 woman, so if I didn't waste too much time I could probably get all the information I needed from her before she got too old to remember anything.

Ruth had lived down the street from us when we were kids. One of my earliest memories was of Ruth burning rubber past our house on her way to church "every time the doors were open," according to my dad, who thought going to church more often than Easter and Christmas was bordering on fanatical. But even when I was a kid and none of us went to church much at all, I sometimes wondered what it would be like to be part of Ruth's big family. Not only did she take her five kids to church with her several times a week, but she also had a full-time job, which was almost unheard-of for moms in those days. I was never quite sure what happened to Ruth's husband, but it was rumored that he "disappeared" a few months after their fifth child was born. That in itself made me think Ruth must be the closest thing to a superwoman that ever existed, since she still seemed to be able to take care of the house and the kids and just about everything else all by herself. The only reason I'd never spent much time around her was that she was always at work or church, and her kids were all boys. I had a brief crush on one of them when I was eight, but when he pinged me on the head with a baseball—from 50 feet, on purpose—I decided he wasn't my type.

Now all those baseball-pinging sons of hers were long gone, and Ruth had taken an early retirement from her secretarial job. My parents now lived hundreds of miles away from Ruth, but Mom stayed in touch with our former neighbor and assured me she still went to church every time the doors were open. Maybe my Proverbs 31 mentor had been living down the street from me all those years, and now might be a good time to visit the old hometown and glean from Ruth's wisdom and experience. When I called to tell her I'd like to make a date to get together for lunch the next time I was in the area, she seemed surprised.

"Why do we need a date? Just drop by anytime. Once a neighbor, always a neighbor."

I'd forgotten that Ruth had a way of speaking her mind, but I imagined she hadn't had much choice but to speak up loud and clear with five boys running around her house.

"Thanks," I said. "I'll do that."

A couple weeks later I made the trip, staying with a friend who still lived in the neighborhood. As I was sitting at the kitchen table one day I said, "I think I'll walk down to Ruth's and see what she's having for lunch."

My friend looked surprised, but before she could comment I said, "I have an open invitation whenever I'm hungry."

Sure enough, Ruth's ancient Ford Escort was parked in her driveway, so I walked to the front door and knocked.

"Come on in," Ruth called through the screen door. "It's not locked."

I couldn't help but wonder if it should be, but then I thought that maybe Ruth's trusting nature was a sign of her spiritual maturity. She'd been a Christian longer than I'd been on this earth, so she'd had more practice trusting God. Feeling encouraged, I opened the door and went inside.

The living room was small but colorful, with splashes of birds and butterflies everywhere—on the wallpaper, the curtains, the sofa, the throw pillows, and even on the afghan draped over the back of the rocker. This lady was really into flying things I decided, blinking my eyes to help clear my vision. I had this unreasonable feeling that flocks of birds and butterflies were going to rise up and swoop over my head at any moment.

Table for Three

"Hello, my dear," Ruth said, walking in from the kitchen and stopping in the middle of the room as she wiped her hands on a dishtowel. I pulled my eyes away from her flighty décor and focused them on the short, stocky woman in front of me. Her salt-and-pepper hair was short and straight, and I doubted she ever bothered with makeup of any kind. But I was pleased to notice that she was wearing plain brown slacks and a tan sweater. It was a relief to see something without wings or feathers, though I was pretty sure I spotted a tiny butterfly pattern on the dishtowel before I averted my eyes.

"I'm just about done fixing our sandwiches," she said. "You can set the table."

How had she known I was coming? I'd called when I arrived a couple of days earlier and told her I'd stop by sometime that week, but I hadn't specified a time. Was she always this ready for whatever came along?

I followed her into the kitchen, where more birds and butterflies greeted me from nearly every square inch of the tiny room. I took a deep breath and did my best not to fixate on all those wings.

"The dishes are in the cupboard right next to you," she barked, her back to me as she spread mayonnaise on a slice of wheat bread. "Make yourself useful. And be sure to set three places."

Still puzzled as to how she knew I was coming and now wondering who else would be joining us, I hesitated.

"Don't just stand there," she said. "The table won't set itself."

I suddenly had a flash of insight into how she managed to work full-time and raise five sons. The thought skittered across my mind that I may have discovered at least part of the reason her husband disappeared, but I dismissed it immediately and scolded myself for being judgmental.

Within minutes the table was set for three, though there were still only two of us in the bird-and-butterfly-infested kitchen. Ruth took her seat and indicated that I should do the same, right across from her, leaving the seat between us vacant. I started to ask who was joining us, but before I could say anything, she bowed her head and closed her eyes. I figured it was my cue to do the same.

"Thank You, Father," Ruth said, her voice softer than usual. "As always, You've provided for us, and we're grateful. Join us here, Lord, as the Head of this household. Amen."

Short, sweet, and to the point, I thought, waiting to open my eyes until I'd raised my head, thereby hoping to avoid looking at the nearly chirping red robin tablecloth and bright yellow butterfly napkins and bluebird plate. I wondered if I could get through my tuna sandwich without looking down.

"I understand you're a believer now," Ruth said, picking up her own sandwich and holding it in front of her face—which, I noted, wasn't nearly as wrinkled as I thought it would be. "You and your mom both. And you're going to a good church. I'm glad. I prayed for you, you know."

I raised my eyebrows in surprise, as she took a bite and started to chew. "I didn't," I said. "Know that you prayed for me, I mean."

She swallowed and nodded. "For your whole family. Every day. Each time I drove by your house or looked out my window and saw one of you walk by. You especially. I knew God had a call on your life."

If I could have raised my eyebrows any higher, I would have. A call on my life? And she knew it when I was a kid? How could a person possibly know something like that about someone else? I wanted to ask, but my mouth was full of tuna fish and wheat bread. Something told me she was experienced at telling people not to talk with their mouths full, so I kept mine shut. Besides, I had this feeling that I could learn a lot more by listening, though I hadn't really had a chance to tell her why I'd come.

"Sometimes life doesn't seem fair," Ruth said, and I wondered where she was going with this golden tidbit of little known information. "That's because it's not. In fact, sometimes it just plain stinks." She took a sip of iced tea and fixed her pale blue eyes on me. "But God..." she said, and then paused as a smile spread across her face, deepening her wrinkles and yet somehow making her look younger. "But God is always there. Always. He doesn't make the problems go away or make an unfair life perfect. But He's there. He's good. And He loves us. That's all that matters."

She glanced at the empty seat between us, and suddenly I understood that when she prayed and invited the Lord to join us for lunch, she meant it. She'd even set a place for Him.

By the time I left an hour or so later, I realized I'd never gotten around to telling Ruth why I was there, and I wasn't sure at that point that she'd be much help to me anyway. As much as I'd admired her when I was little, I could see now that she was an average, normal person like anyone else—a little eccentric and quirky, maybe, but normal. And I needed more than normal or average when it came to learning how to run a tight ship.

Still, I came away from our visit feeling like I'd learned something, even if I couldn't quite put my finger on what it was. Maybe one day, after I'd found my Proverbs 31 mentor and discovered all I needed to know to become spiritually mature, I'd visit Ruth again—assuming she was still alive by then—and ask her why she had such a fascination with flying things. But I wouldn't ask her why she set the extra place at her table. I was pretty sure it had something to do with why she was able to take care of the house and her job and all five kids after her husband disappeared.

 Making It Personal

Can you think of someone in your past who made a lasting and positive impression on you? What character traits and qualities did that person have? What was their relationship with Christ like? If you could sit down with that person right now, what questions would you ask, and why?

And my God shall supply all your need according to His riches in glory by Christ Jesus.
—Philippians 4:19

FOOD COURT FIASCO

3

I'd learned some things but still had two strikes against me, so I wanted to take a little break before choosing another candidate. I decided to do something I almost never do— I went shopping.

Seriously, shopping is not my thing. Yeah, I know, I should have realized right then I'd never achieve my superwoman goal. Without the shopping gene, I didn't have a chance. But I was young and optimistic, and I needed a change of pace and scenery to think things through. So, minus kids, friends, husband, mom, or anyone else, I headed for the mall.

I hadn't been there more than five minutes—most of which had been spent standing in front of the Fudge Forever Factory, trying to talk myself out of going inside—when I heard a familiar voice.

"Kathi? Is that you?"

I didn't have to turn around to know it was Bernadine Johnson, the bane of my existence for as long as I could remember. Bernadine, whose size made it inevitable that we kids, in our foolish grammar school humor, would rename her "Big Bertha" but whose permanent disconnect with reality seemed to make her oblivious to the fact that we had done so, had found me. Was it a coincidence that our reunion was about to take place in front of the candy store? I doubted it.

I sighed and turned to face her. Sure enough, it was Bernadine—big-as-ever Bernadine, smiling ear-to-ear as if she expected me to be as happy about seeing her as she obviously was about seeing me.

Wait a minute! Was that any attitude for a Christian to take toward an unbeliever? Poor Bernadine was clueless—or so I thought—about her size, about our so-called friendship, and most important, about eternity. Could this be a divine appointment, one of those look-whom-I-placed-in-your-path-to-witness-to occasions? If so, then everything I'd heard about God having a sense of humor must be true. I mean, Bernadine Johnson, of all people!

I smiled—the least I could do under the circumstances. "Hi, Bernadine," I managed to say. "How are you?"

Though I saw it with my own eyes, I still couldn't believe it. Bernadine's smile actually widened!

"I'm fine," she gushed, her blue eyes dancing as she rushed forward and enveloped me in a hug. "And how are you? It's so good to see you!"

I wanted to answer but she'd temporarily cut off my air supply, so I nodded and did my best to extricate myself. When she released me I started breathing again and gasped, "Fine...thanks," glancing around to see how many shoppers had witnessed our dramatic embrace. Thankfully, the mall was relatively empty that day, and the few people who did happen to be in our vicinity were busy with their own pursuits.

"So what are you doing here?" Bernadine asked, still grinning. "I thought you didn't like shopping. You never used to. But I haven't seen you in a couple of years, and I heard a lot of things have changed with you. Is that true?"

Oh, boy, was it ever! But how did I tell her the changes were about something a lot more important than my aversion to shopping? *Help me, God! I haven't done this before.*

"Um, well, yeah," I said, no doubt impressing her with my brilliant vocabulary. Was that the best I could do? I was going to have to increase my efforts at finding a Proverbs 31 role model and get some serious help—fast!

"Why don't we get a couple of diet sodas and find somewhere to sit down and talk?" Bernadine's suggestion caught me by surprise for two reasons—one, that it had the word "diet" in it, and two, that she was the one making it instead of me. Regardless, the suggestion was a good one. I nodded in agreement and we walked to the first available fast-food outlet and ordered our drinks, then found an empty bench and settled down for what I hoped would be a brilliant evangelistic offering on my part.

"So tell me about it," Bernadine said, sipping her soda and looking at me with what appeared to be genuine interest. "What's been going on in your life?"

Shooting another quick prayer skyward, I decided to start out easy, giving her a brief family update before moving on. When I ran out of information and still felt hesitant about jumping into my first turn-or-burn sermon, I decided to ask about her life. Showing interest in others was the mature thing to do, something I was sure the Proverbs 31 woman would have done.

Bernadine smiled again and said, "Not much new in my corner of the world. It's just me and my two cats—and my bookkeeping job."

For as long as I had known her—which went all the way back to kindergarten—Bernadine had liked numbers. She once told me it was because numbers were predictable and constant. There was something to be said for that, I supposed.

And that was it. She was done. Nothing more to say. We were back to me and the changes in my life since I'd last seen her. OK, ready or not...

Faithful Witness or Mighty Mouse Jr.?

"I'm a Christian now." There. I'd said it—not too eloquently, but it was a start.

"So I heard." Her smile still showed, but a questioning lift had been added to one corner of it, and her eyes had narrowed slightly. "I ran into your mom one day, and she told me you were into the church-thing."

Aha. So that's what this was about. The church-thing, huh? As if Miss Bernadine Johnson had ever darkened the door of any church anywhere at any time.

I decided I'd better correct her before either of us said another word. "It's not a church-thing," I said, forcing myself to return her ever-present-and-getting-more-annoying-by-the-moment smile. "It's a Jesus-thing. I—"

"So you're a Jesus freak," she interrupted. "I've heard of them. Lots of long-hairs, getting baptized in the ocean, sitting around playing guitars and singing and claiming to be born again."

My smile was fading fast, and my irritation factor was on the rise. "That's because we are—born again, that is. That's what happens when you repent, and—"

This time she actually rolled her eyes, though she managed to maintain her smile. "Ah," she said, "the 'r' word. I knew that would come up sooner or later."

If she knew I was going to say it and she didn't want to hear it, why did she go out of her way to get me to talk about it? "I'm just trying to explain what happened to me," I said, keeping my voice calm and even, while repeating silently to myself, *Proverbs 31 woman, Proverbs 31 woman.* "That's what you asked me, isn't it?"

Her smile faded a notch. "You're right," she admitted with a shrug. "I just didn't think you were going to preach at me and tell me what a sinner I was."

Where did that come from? Bernadine obviously had more of a self-image problem than I'd realized. All I wanted to do was tell her how wonderful Jesus was and give her the opportunity to accept Him as her Savior, just as I had. Why couldn't she understand that?

Maybe I wasn't making myself clear enough.

"Bernadine," I said, my attempt to maintain a smile long-since forgotten, "you need Jesus. You need to be born again. You need to get saved."

Now her smile was gone too, and her face went from pale to paler, as neither of us spoke and our eyes locked. Finally she spoke. "*Saved*? I need to get *saved*?"

Before I could answer, she burst into laughter—very loud laughter, I might add—and more than a couple of heads turned in our direction.

"That's right. The Bible says—"

Now she was laughing even louder, and her face was no longer pale. In fact, it was edging toward red, and I wondered if otherwise healthy but extremely chubby twentysomethings ever dropped dead of heart attacks from laughing too hard. I certainly hoped not, as the otherwise healthy but extremely chubby twentysomething who sat laughing hysterically in front of me was definitely not ready to meet her Maker.

Finally, wiping the tears from her eyes and fighting to catch her breath, Bernadine gasped, "Oh, Kathi, you always did remind me of Mighty Mouse."

Mighty Mouse? What was that supposed to mean?

"You know," she said, still giggling, then breaking into song, "*Here I come to save the day!*" She took another breath and said, "Always the superhero, wanting to rescue the world. Now you're a Jesus freak, wanting to save the world one soul at a time. Oh, this is too funny!"

I didn't think it was funny at all, but two teenagers sitting at a nearby bench must have thought so because they too were laughing, and I was sure Bernadine and I were the source of their amusement. This conversation was going nowhere fast—and it was all my fault. God had given me a golden opportunity to introduce Bernadine to Jesus, and I'd blown it. My quest to become a spiritual superwoman was hopeless.

I stood to my feet and gazed down at Bernadine, still smirking and snorting, though it was obvious she was trying to restrain herself. "I'm sorry," I said, "but I have to go. I…"

The words stuck in my throat; I swallowed, but it didn't help, so I spun on my heel and marched away as quickly as I could, the laughter of Bernadine and two anonymous teens fueling my tears of frustration and failure. The worst part was that I couldn't decide if I was more upset because I hadn't been able to get through to Bernadine—or because she had gotten to me with her all-too-accurate description of my lifelong desire to be a superhero.

Would I ever find the answer to becoming the Proverbs 31 woman I so longed to be, or would I forever be dodging loose cannons? A lightning bolt of thought zigzagged through my brain, telling me I'd just moved a fraction of an inch closer to my goal—in spite of myself—but I dismissed it as quickly as it came. My only hope was to find the wise woman who would be my role model and teach me what I needed to know before Bernadine and the rest of the unsaved world really did go to hell in the proverbial handbasket.

 Making It Personal

Have you ever felt as if you'd blown it when trying to tell someone about Jesus? Why do you suppose you felt that way? Have you considered that seemingly unsuccessful attempts are a natural part of spiritual growth? If confronted with the same situation today, how would you handle it?

● ● ● ● ●

So shall My word be that goes forth from My mouth; it shall not return to Me void, but it shall accomplish what I please, and it shall prosper in the thing for which I sent it.
—Isaiah 55:11

THE WOMAN WITH 97 CHILDREN

4

A few days later I attended a volunteer appreciation tea at my youngest son's preschool, still brooding about my failure to evangelize Bernadine and wondering if I'd ever find someone qualified to be my mentor. It was a given that I wouldn't find that person in this secular school gathering, but I was determined to present a good Christian witness to everyone present, despite my inner misgivings about my qualifications.

I sipped the tepid tea in the lovely floral cup as one of the teachers—presumably the "designated speaker" because she was the only person in the room not drinking tea—droned on about how much we were appreciated and how the school couldn't function without dedicated volunteers. I thought of the many hours I'd spent there, wiping runny noses and comforting crying three-year-olds who wanted to know when Mommy was coming back, and I had to admit I was happy to do my part, though I failed to see how it could possibly help propel me toward my ultimate goal of achieving spiritual superwoman status. I breathed a sigh of relief as the speaker wrapped up her comments and invited us to get to know one another, being sure to sample the sugar cookies that had been baked and decorated by our precious progeny.

"Bring me a couple of those red ones, will you, child?" The shaky voice to my right snagged my attention as a bony hand clutched my arm.

Surprised, I turned to meet the owner of the shaky voice, the bony hand, and the old-fashioned white lace glove that covered the hand. Set in a coffee-colored, wrinkled face, the dark eyes that stared back at me were clouded and rheumy, though I quickly forgot about her advanced age as I saw the sparkle of wisdom and mischief that danced behind her cataracts.

"Excuse me?" I said, trying to bring into focus what she'd asked of me just seconds earlier.

"The red ones. They're my favorites."

When I still didn't get it and the look on my face no doubt reflected my confusion, she smiled and nodded toward the table against the wall. "The cookies with the red sprinkles. Bring me two. I never eat more than two because I'm not supposed to have too much sugar, but one's never enough. I never eat any of the others. Just the red ones. Two of them. Please."

Apparently she considered that sufficient explanation to require my compliance with her request, and I suppose it was because the next thing I knew I was standing in front of the cookie table, placing two sugar cookies with red sprinkles on a plate for my elegantly dressed new acquaintance. I grabbed a couple extra cookies—red ones, of course—for myself and returned to my seat.

The lady with the sparkling eyes and the immaculate white gloves, not to mention the pillbox hat that sat atop her short, frizzy white hair, was smiling. I smiled back as I placed her two red cookies on the table and sat down beside her.

"They had quite a variety of different colored cookies over there," I commented. "Why do you just eat the red ones?"

She stopped chewing and looked at me as if I'd suggested she jump up on the table and do the cancan. "I only eat the red ones," she said, her voice slowing to emphasize the distinct single syllables of her statement: "Just-the-red-ones."

Aha. No sense pursuing this conversation. I'd eat my cookies and excuse myself to go find someone who wasn't quite so opposed to variety—although I had to admit that the red cookies really were good. My mouth was full of them when my neighbor laid her hand on my arm again. I looked up. Her penciled-in eyebrows were raised curiously.

"How many children do you have here at the preschool?" she asked.

Chewing faster and gulping what was left of my now room-temperature tea so I wouldn't choke while swallowing, I finally managed to say, "One. Only one. My other children are in grammar school."

She smiled and nodded, apparently approving of my answer. "I have 97," she said.

This time my own eyebrows shot up. Ninety-seven? Obviously she considered every student at the school to be hers. I smiled.

"That's nice. I think it's wonderful that you come and volunteer your time, especially at your—" I caught myself. Would she be offended if I implied that she was a bit old for volunteering at a preschool? Somehow I couldn't imagine her, in her white gloves and pillbox hat, wiping runny noses or rolling "snakes" with homemade peanut-butter-dough clay.

Her laughter tinkled, and I relaxed as she spoke. "Especially at my age? Is that what you were going to say, child? Well, don't you worry none about hurting old Cora's feelings. Why, I been on this here earth so long I'm way past that. If I still got my feelings hurt over every thoughtless thing people say, I'd miss out on all the joy."

I'd never thought about life quite like that before, but I hadn't lived as long as Cora. Would I one day be old and mature enough to ignore the hurtful things people said and just experience the joy?

Covered

"What exactly is it you do here?" I asked. "Do you volunteer in one particular classroom, or...?"

"I cover 'em all."

"All of them? You mean, you go to every one of the classrooms and spend time with the kids, helping the teachers...?" My voice trailed off, as I imagined this frail but genteel lady hobbling from class to class and helping in each one. In all the times I'd been at the school, I didn't remember seeing her there. How was that possible?

"Actually," she said, breaking off a corner of her cookie, "I only come to the school one day a year—on volunteer appreciation day—so I can get my two red cookies."

This conversation was getting weirder by the minute. Why couldn't I sit next to another mom, someone with whom I could converse about potty training and sibling rivalry and...well, all the normal everyday stuff that went with the current territory of my existence? I had to settle in next to the female version of Methuselah, who believed she "covered" an entire school with her once-a-year appearance at which she ate her two red cookies and then left.

The story of my life. I'm looking for a mentor, someone to teach me about being a Proverbs 31 woman, and what do I find? An eccentric old woman who doesn't have a clue what's going on!

I was about to get up and leave when she said, "How can I cover you, child?"

I blinked. What was this crazy old woman talking about now? Cover me? What was that supposed to mean? How was I supposed to answer a question like that?

My eyes darted around the room, hoping someone would be near enough for me to make eye contact so I could excuse myself to go speak with someone other than the ancient cookie monster who now wanted to "cover" me. Unfortunately, most everyone else had grabbed their cookies and gone home. I made a mental note to be sure to do that if I was there for next year's tea.

"Surely there's something you'd like me to pray about for you," Cora said, her hat bobbing as she nodded. "We all need prayer, you know."

So that's what she meant—covering me with prayer! I felt a little embarrassed. That's what she'd meant about covering the whole school. She prayed for these kids—all of them—and the teachers too, no doubt.

"I had no idea that anyone was praying for these kids," I said. "How long have you been doing that?"

"For as long as I can remember," she said, and then winked. "The problem is, some days I remember a lot, and some days I don't. But whatever else I forget, I always remember to pray for these kids and their families, and for the teachers too. At my age, that's about all I can do, but it's what God told me to do, so that's enough. He said this school is my assignment, so the first thing every morning when I get out of bed, I get down on my knees and ask the good Lord to bless and protect these little ones so they can grow up to love Jesus like I do."

I was so excited to realize God had assigned someone to pray for a secular school! It was a new concept for me, and I found myself wondering how many other schools and businesses had prayer covering assigned to them by God—whether anyone knew it or not.

"Who else knows about this?" I asked. "Are the teachers aware of your assignment?"

Cora's laughter tinkled again, and I realized how young her eyes appeared when she laughed. "Some of them do. They're the ones who make sure I'm invited to the tea so I can get my red cookies." She shrugged. "Other than that, I suppose only God knows."

Only God knows. I knew in my heart that was all that mattered, and yet it seemed this dedicated woman should get some sort of special recognition or thanks—at least something more than a couple of red cookies each year. But she seemed perfectly content to leave things as they were.

"You look puzzled, child," she said, frowning a bit. "Is something wrong?"

I shook my head. "I was just thinking...how are these people going to know about Jesus unless you tell them? Praying is wonderful—the most important thing there is—but wouldn't it be nice if you could stand up in front of this group of volunteers and tell them what you do? Not to gain personal recognition, but so you could present the gospel to them or at least explain why you do what you do so they can ask questions if they want to know more. It seems like a great opportunity to evangelize."

Cora smiled. "St. Francis of Assisi said, 'Preach the Gospel at all times and when necessary use words.' I have found his advice to be quite helpful through the years."

I had no response for that one. By the time I left the tea, I'd given my list of prayer requests to Cora and had received one from her as well. I may not have had time to go out looking for my Proverbs 31 role model that day, but at least I'd found a new prayer partner—and I'd learned something about the importance of letting my life do the preaching. Somehow I sensed that newfound knowledge might be helpful as I continued to dodge all those loose cannons.

 Making It Personal

Have you ever felt "ambushed" by a chance encounter, only to discover the meeting was really a divine appointment? What did you learn from that appointment, and how has it changed your life? How have you been able to pass along to someone else the life lessons you learned from that meeting?

• • • • •

Do not let your beauty be merely outward—arranging the hair, wearing gold, or putting on fine apparel—rather let it be the hidden person of the heart, with the incorruptible beauty of a gentle and quiet spirit, which is very precious in the sight of God.
—1 Peter 3:3–4

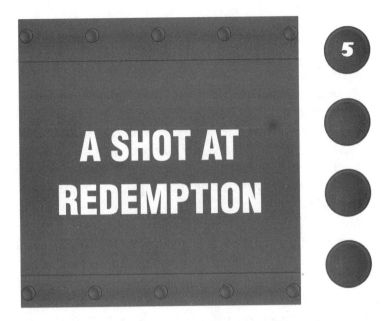

A SHOT AT REDEMPTION

I thought about Cora over the next few days and kept her prayer requests in the front of my Bible so I wouldn't forget to pray for her every morning. Knowing she was praying for me became a great source of encouragement, as I continued to ask God to help me in my quest to become like the Proverbs 31 woman.

But sometimes life got too busy to worry about achieving my goal. There were days when it was all I could do to remember to brush my teeth in the morning and put gas in the car before leaving for town. This was one of those days when I forgot—not to brush my teeth but to put gas in the car. It was also my day to volunteer at the preschool where I'd met Cora. As a result, Chris, my youngest, and I were late, since the auto club was backed up on emergency calls that took priority over an unorganized mother and an upset three-year-old waiting on the side of the road.

"Mom, let's go," Chris whined, his as yet undiagnosed ADHD (attention deficit hyperactivity disorder) kicking in as he bounced on the backseat. "I want to go to school, Mom! Mom, let's go! Mom!"

Likely just seconds before my head exploded, the cavalry showed up, and in a matter of minutes we were back on the road and racing to our destination—which was not a good idea because we soon had to pull over again, this time due to the flashing red lights and wailing siren immediately behind us.

By the time we finally arrived, Chris had missed snack time and was not a happy camper—nor were the two ladies trying to ride herd on 23 spinning, squealing preschoolers. Chris, already in his spinning, squealing mode, jumped right into the fray.

"Where have you been?" Jeannie, the other volunteer, demanded the minute she saw me. "We really needed you. We have two extra kids today—visitors—and..."

"I'm sorry," I said, haphazardly hanging my jacket on the already-full coat closet hooks. It slipped right off, but before I could pick it up and try again, Jeannie grabbed my arm and said, "Come on. We've got to try to settle them down for story time." We began to peel kids off the ceiling and walls and nudge them toward the story circle where we hoped they would sit quietly and listen for 10 or 15 minutes.

Miss McDougall, the teacher of these pint-sized tornadoes, joined us. "It's like trying to organize a bunch of earthworms, isn't it?" she asked. I grunted, unable to say more as I made my way to the circle, a child attached to each hand and one wrapped around my leg. The worst of the shrieking seemed to be coming from one last rebel in the far corner, who refused to join the group until he got his snack.

Of course, it was Chris. I sighed, resisting the impulse to abandon the majority of the group that had finally assembled in the circle and instead go drag my child by the scruff of the neck to his proper place and insist he settle down and behave. Wisely, I allowed Jeannie to coax him over with an orange slice and a promise of more when story time was over.

Not only was I failing as a spiritual superwoman, I wasn't even a passable mother. I could at least get up early enough to make sure my child had a nutritious breakfast before causing him to be late for snack time. *No more procrastinating when it comes to putting gas in the car*, I thought as I lowered myself to the floor and folded my legs in front of me. *Or anything else for that matter! From now on I'm getting everything ready the night before....*

Nathan, with his curly blond hair and chubby cheeks, climbed onto my lap and immediately stuck his thumb in his mouth and snuggled up against me. I smiled in spite of myself. Whatever other failings I might have, this particular not-quite-three-year-old had taken an immediate liking to me the first day I volunteered in the classroom, and he never missed a chance to sit on my lap. Maybe I was doing at least one thing right.

As Miss McDougall read the story, periodically holding up the book so everyone could see the pictures, I sat back and enjoyed the warmth of Nathan's little thumb-sucking body nestled against mine as I scanned the rest of the group. Chris had settled in on Jeannie's right side and was meticulously extracting every last bit of juice out of his paltry orange-slice breakfast while glaring at me across the circle as if I were purposely trying to starve him. It was obvious he was sticking to Jeannie like glue until he got the rest of his promised snack, whatever that might be. Good thing he didn't have to depend on me to keep him nourished between now and lunchtime, as the only bite-sized morsels I had lurking around the bottom of my purse were a couple of lint-coated cough drops and a loose button or two. There was a time when each of my sons would have popped those pathetic offerings right into their mouths, sending me into a Heimlich-maneuver frenzy, but thankfully those days were over.

Melanie, an almost four-year-old and therefore slightly more mature than the other dark-haired beauties sitting next to me, tugged at my sleeve. "Miss Kathi," she whispered. "Miss Kathi, Nathan's—"

"Shh," I whispered, smiling down at her. "Miss McDougall is reading right now. You can tell me later."

"But, Miss Kathi—"

I shook my head. "Later," I repeated, using my kindest but firmest tone. The least I could do was help teach those little ones about manners: in this case, if someone is talking, don't interrupt. I smiled again and turned my eyes to the teacher, determined to set a good example. I heard Melanie sigh, as Miss McDougall finished her story and asked if there were any questions.

A shy little girl named Maureen, whose mother had just had a baby, raised her hand. "Where was Bunny Rabbit's baby sister?" she asked, raising a chorus of giggles.

Patiently, Miss McDougall explained that not every family has a baby sister or brother, which seemed to surprise Maureen and satisfy her curiosity as well.

What a Surprise

After a couple more questions, Miss McDougall reminded the class that we had a visitor that day—an aunt who had brought her two young nephews to check out our school. "As I told you earlier, class"—obviously while Chris and I were languishing on the side of the roadway—"please make our visitors feel welcome, and include Daniel and Marcus in your games."

I started to turn my head to locate the aunt who had brought her nephews to check out the school, but Melanie raised her hand, jumping in with a question before Miss McDougall could excuse the children to go play.

"Teacher, why is Nathan doing that? My mom says it's not nice."

All conversation ceased, and all eyes turned toward Nathan—and consequently settled on me, where Nathan was sitting.

I looked down as Nathan looked up, his right index finger firmly inserted into his right nostril. I was sure he'd been sucking his thumb when the story started, but apparently he had changed digits and orifices at some point during the story—no doubt just as Melanie tried to alert me to the problem. I pulled Nathan's right arm away from his face, effectively unplugging his nostril and silently thanking God that the situation had been brought to our attention before the little guy returned to thumb-sucking... or worse.

I shuddered and jumped up, carrying Nathan to the bathroom to get a tissue for his nose and to wash his hands. Once again the chorus of giggles made its way around the circle, but Nathan didn't seem to mind. He was perfectly content to let me carry him while I enforced a safe distance between his right hand and his mouth. Through it all, he grinned up at me, blue eyes shining, as if I were the love of his life.

Before I knew it, my three hours were up—though I'd actually been there less than two hours because Chris and I had been so late. I was about to gather my son from the pile of screaming block-builders on the far side of the room and my jacket from the coat closet floor when I heard a familiar voice.

"Kathi?"

I stopped. That voice—it sounded like... No, it couldn't be. What would she be doing here—in a preschool of all places?

I turned. Sure enough, it was Bernadine Johnson, waiting near the door with Daniel and Marcus. I had forgotten all about the preschool's visitor.

"Bernadine?" My eyebrows drew together in a puzzled frown. "I didn't know..."

Bernadine smiled. "Didn't know I had nephews? Don't you remember my little sister, Flo? She got married right out of high school, and these are her kids. She had to go back to work recently, and since I had some vacation time coming, I offered to watch the kids while I try to help her find a good day care. I didn't know you worked here."

"Oh, I don't. I'm just a volunteer—you know, for a few hours a week. My son loves it here."

Bernadine's smile widened as her eyes darted toward the noisy male gathering where I had last seen Chris. "I saw you two come in earlier. Your son looks... busy."

I felt the heat creep into my cheeks. "That's one way to describe him. Maybe I should say he keeps me busy."

Bernadine laughed, as her nephews tugged on her hands and started firing one-word demands at her like "hamburger" and "ice cream."

"I think I'm learning about busy," she said. "Listen, can we talk some time? I know I was rude to you at the mall the other day, but..." She took a deep breath before continuing. "I really do want to talk to you about the things you were trying to tell me—you know, about Jesus and repenting and all that."

"You do? But why? I didn't even stick around to talk much that day, and—"

Bernadine shrugged. "It's not so much what you said or didn't say that got me curious. It was the way you didn't get mad at me for being such a jerk. And the way you were with the kids today. I realized you were—I don't know. Different, I guess. That's what I want to talk to you about."

Preach the Gospel at all times, and when necessary use words.

Cora's wise advice echoed in my mind, and I smiled. Maybe I was making progress after all.

 Making It Personal

What times in your life have you felt like a failure, only to find encouragement from the least likely source? Can you think of times when you've been a source of unexpected encouragement to someone else? Is there someone who might need some encouragement today? How can you extend the hand of Jesus to offer that encouragement?

And let us not grow weary while doing good, for in due season we shall reap if we do not lose heart.
—Galatians 6:9

LEARNING TO WALK— SLOW AND SHAKY, BUT ON MY FEET

If you think you are standing firm, be careful that you don't fall.
—1 Corinthians 10:12 (NIV)

Baby Steps

What About Bob? is one of the funniest movies I've ever seen. I've laughed my way through it many times, which is highly unusual for me, as it's a rare film that holds my interest more than once. I've asked myself what it is about this particular movie that intrigues me—beyond the obvious, which is that it's a story about an over-the-edge neurotic who carries his goldfish in a water pouch around his neck and endears himself to his therapist's family through his eccentric but winsome ways, even as he infuriates the therapist and eventually drives him over the edge. As humorous as that is, the most memorable part of the movie is a simple two-word phrase: "baby steps."

When Bob learns his therapist is going on vacation and won't be able to see him for a while, the poor man is panic-stricken. He informs the doctor that he simply cannot function that long without him, so the therapist advises him not to be overwhelmed by the situation but to approach it with "baby steps." We then see Bob proceeding through the movie, reminding himself at every juncture: "Baby steps, baby steps, baby steps..."

For those of us who are parents, there are few memories that equal watching our offspring take their first baby steps. Our oldest son, Al, was a typical firstborn. He took his first steps before he was nine months old, and as soon as he realized he was mobile, there was no stopping him. Our second son, Michael, was just the opposite. He much preferred to sit in one spot and point at what he wanted, fully expecting that his older brother would bring it to him, which he usually did; although as they got older Al often used the retrieved object to hit Michael over the head before handing it to him. Michael was nearly 15 months old before he took his first baby steps, though I don't doubt he could have walked long before. He simply saw no reason to do so. Chris, the baby of the family, was more like Al and walked before he was a year.

Regardless of when our children took their first baby steps, they all had one thing in common: The rug rats had become toddlers, and toddlers fall down...a lot. Then they cry and holler until the nearest grown-up shows the proper sympathy for the newest boo-boo. This seemed to work best for Al, since parents are always more concerned when the firstborn cries. By the time the second child comes along, the parents' scream reactor has been toned down. While the first child gets lots of hugs and kisses and "poor baby" comments, followed by cookies and milk, the second gets a quick once-over to make sure there are no injuries requiring a trip to the emergency room, then a quick kiss on the forehead and a perfunctory "You're fine, sweetheart; now go play." When the third one takes a spill and considers hollering for sympathy, he takes a quick inventory of the available adults, all deeply ensconced in their own activities, and decides it's not worth the effort, since previous responses to his cries have amounted to little more than a cursory glance in the fallen child's direction.

As a Christian, I was beginning to realize that my spiritual walk had a lot of similarities to the different stages of childhood. When I became a born-again believer at the age of 26, my excitement and enthusiasm far outweighed my wisdom and discretion. I was a baby Christian, a spiritual rug rat who spent most of my time on my knees, learning the basics, such as how to crawl from point A to point B. But I had outgrown that stage a couple years back. I was now on my feet, a "spiritual toddler," learning to walk and making progress toward achieving my goal of becoming a Proverbs 31 spiritual superwoman. I might still fall on occasion, but I had also discovered that Micah 7:8 declares, "When I fall, I will arise." That verse had been added to my favorite faith-building scriptures. Whatever I still had to learn to become a mature Christian, I was confident I would learn it quickly. Soon, out of my own reservoir of accumulated wisdom, I would begin to teach and lead others—humbly, of course.

I could hardly wait to get started....

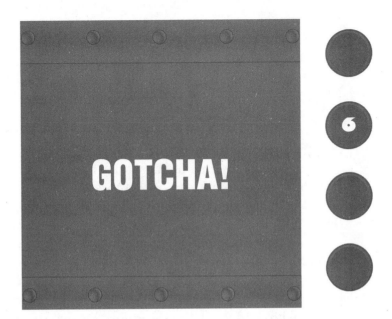

GOTCHA!

Until I sat down to try to explain to someone about Jesus and repentance and the need to be born again, I truly believed there was no experience so awesome as becoming a mother. But when, not long after our preschool encounter, I actually led Bernadine to the place of praying to receive Jesus as her Savior and being born into the Kingdom of God—in my own bumbling way and all while we sat on the grass at the park with my son and her nephews playing nearby—I realized I'd been wrong. Becoming a sort of spiritual mother by helping to facilitate someone's birth into God's family is at least as exciting, if not more so, than birthing your own physical child into the world.

If I'd had any sense I would have carried the analogy to the next level. With all the experience I had at changing dirty diapers and living on 15 minutes of sleep a day, I shouldn't have been surprised that spiritual newborns are just as messy, demanding, and self-absorbed as physical ones. But scarcely being beyond that stage myself, the connection never occurred to me—which is why I was so surprised when Bernadine kept showing up on my doorstep with questions I couldn't answer.

"Which is the right way to be baptized—sprinkling or dunking—and why?"

"If the Hebrew word 'Sabbath' means Saturday or 'the last day of the week,' how did our day of worship get changed to Sunday?"

"What's the difference between pre-trib, mid-trib, and post-trib, and which do you think is right?"

"Do you believe in a literal six-day creation period, and if so, how does evolution fit in—or does it?"

"What's the significance of the Urim and Thummim?" (Huh???)

I had helped to create a "monster"—one with a voracious appetite to read and study the Bible and to ask lots of questions. Actually, this would have been a good thing if the person she was asking had been a Christian long enough to answer with confidence. But she was dealing with yours truly, who had yet to find the perfect Proverbs 31 role model, and my confidence level regarding the finer points of theology was definitely one of the looser cannons on my deck of life. I'd been listening to sermons and going to Sunday school for a couple of years by then, but I realized when I tried to answer Bernadine's questions that I was just repeating what I'd heard someone else say. When she took a question to the next level—"What did the pastor mean when he said he believes in a literal millennium, and do you agree with him?"—I was stumped.

This should have been another clue that I had a long way to go in my own spiritual walk; instead, it just irritated me and made me wish Bernadine would quit hanging around so much. The newfound glow of spiritual motherhood was beginning to fade.

Then one morning while I was volunteering at the preschool and helping to supervise the kids on the playground, Chris—who insisted he was "almost four," though his birthday was still eight months away—came running up to me with a panicky look on his flushed face.

"Help me! Those kids are after me!"

My mama bear instinct kicked in as I began scanning the playground for the bullies who had threatened my cub. Imagine my surprise when the only ones chasing him were three little girls, none of whom could have been more than two and a half. As they charged toward us, giggling and squealing, Chris ducked behind me and did his best to become invisible. (Actually, it wasn't that hard. He weighed thirty pounds soaking wet, and I was still carrying those extra "baby fat" pounds I'd put on before he was born—all of which had somehow settled on my hips.) Unfortunately for Chris, my "wide glide" didn't do him any good, as the girls darted behind me and spotted their prey.

"Chris! We found you! Come and play with us!"

"I don't want to," Chris whined, his voice muffled as he wrapped his arms around my right thigh. "Leave me alone!"

"Chris," I said, peeling him off me, "what's wrong with you? The girls just want to play."

My son glared up at me as if I'd agreed to sell him into slavery. "I don't want to play with them. They're pests, and they bug me!"

"That's not nice," I said in my most authoritative tone. "You shouldn't say that about anyone. Apologize to the girls."

He shook his head. "Not until you do."

I frowned. "Why should I apologize to the girls?"

Busted

By that time the veins were popping out on my son's forehead and neck, and he answered, "Not them, Mom. Your friend. You know, Marcus and Daniel's aunt. The one that comes over all the time, the one who you sometimes hide from so she'll go away."

"Chris," I said, trying to maintain my calm, even as I felt my face going red-hot, "that's not the same. Bernadine is—"

"She's a pest," he insisted. "You said so. And you said she bugs you. I heard you—when you were hiding in the kitchen when she rang the doorbell. Remember?"

I did remember. I looked from Chris to the girls, who stood staring up at me, their eyes wide, waiting to see how I would deal with my son's unacceptable behavior.

I was waiting to see the same thing. How was I going to handle this situation, especially since I knew Chris was right? That was the worst part—being busted by an "almost four-year-old" in front of three of his only slightly younger peers.

"You're right," I said, swallowing my shattered pride along with the growing lump in my throat. "I do owe Bernadine an apology. Thank you for pointing that out."

Chris's eyebrows shot up, as it dawned on him that he had just pulled off a coup that could easily set him up as the godfather of the playground once word got out—and neither of us had any doubt that our audience of three would make sure it did. I realized it was up to me to head things off at the pass.

"You're right that I owe Bernadine an apology, and I will call her when we get home and take care of that. But for now, you need to apologize too. If you don't want to play with the girls, fine." I stopped and looked over at the deflated trio, whose shoulders sagged at my pronouncement, and then turned my attention back to Chris. "But calling them pests and saying they bug you is not fine. For that you need to apologize."

Now it was time for Chris's shoulders to sag. He gave me one last glance of appeal, but I nixed it with a shake of my head. He sighed. "Sorry," he whispered.

"A little louder, please."

He sighed again. "Sorry."

"What are you sorry about?"

"Calling them names," he mumbled.

"And why are you sorry?"

Our eyes locked in a brief battle of wills, but he finally gave in. "Because it isn't nice."

I looked back at the girls, who seemed stunned by the turn of events. "Girls, Chris has apologized to you. Can you tell him you forgive him?"

They nodded in unison as their singsong voices pronounced absolution.

"Good. Now, go play. Next time you want someone to play with you, just ask. If they say no, then respect that and leave them alone. Understood?"

They nodded again, their eyes growing wider as they realized that they too had been reprimanded. Then, as if on cue, they scampered away.

"Are you really going to tell Bernadine you're sorry?" Chris asked, still staring after the girls.

"I really am."

He stood there a moment, and then, apparently satisfied, nodded and went off to find some "guy stuff" to do.

I, on the other hand, was not looking forward to fulfilling my promise—though I knew I had no choice. God had orchestrated an example that was too clear to ignore. Three little girls, more than a bit overzealous and demanding in their self-absorbed quest for attention, being rejected by one only slightly older than them and labeled as "pests"—the correlation was just too obvious.

When I called Bernadine, she was much more gracious than I could have hoped. She admitted she'd always known I'd considered her a pest.

"You weren't the only one. Even my mom called me a pest. She was always telling me to leave her alone and go find something to do. So I'd usually just go eat something. I suppose that's why there's so much of me to love."

She paused, but before I could think of something appropriate to say, she added, "Seriously, Kathi, I know I can get on people's nerves. I don't mean to, but... I just do. But it's different with God. I know I never get on His nerves, or bug Him, or make Him wish I'd go away and find something else to do. No matter what, He's always there for me, and that's the best part about being a Christian."

No matter what. Bernadine was right. But who would have thought I'd be chastised with such a great truth from a baby Christian? I knew she didn't mean it as a criticism, but I was humbled by the timely reminder.

Bernadine and I bonded through that experience, as we recognized our mutual need for discipleship. We were both in the very early stages of our Christian life—rug rats and toddlers learning to walk—and though our heavenly Father was the only One who could ultimately grow us up, we also recognized our need for other believers to help us along the way—to model the correct way to walk, to pick us up when we fell, and to cheer us on as we took each step.

While I felt as if I'd dodged a loose cannon this time I knew there were more to come....

 ## Making It Personal

Think back to when you were a new Christian. Who helped you? Have you ever become irritated by someone you consider a pest—a person who bugged you with constant questions and demands for your time? In light of my experience at the preschool, can you see those demanding people in a different light? In what ways can you set proper limits, while still making yourself available to help fellow believers grow in their walk with the Lord?

And this commandment we have from Him: that he who loves God must love his brother also.
—1 John 4:21

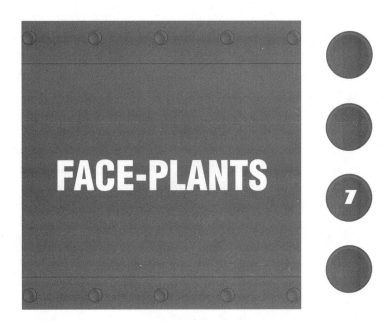

FACE-PLANTS

7

My author friend Ginny Smith likes to ski. She talks of swooshing gracefully down snow-covered mountains, while I shiver at the mere thought—as much out of fear as from the imagined cold. Ginny also talks about *face-plants*, a term used by skiers when their ski tips get crossed and they land facedown in the cold snow. Sounds painful, as well as uncomfortable—which could be one of the reasons I'm discussing Ginny's skiing experiences and not my own. The term *face-plant* is enough to keep me from trying my hand (or feet) at something as precarious and foolhardy as strapping on two long pieces of polished wood and then pushing myself down the side of a mountain.

In reference to face-plants, Ginny goes on to explain that each time she ends up in such a position, she turns it into a positive experience, because the fall teaches her to be more focused when she gets up and proceeds on her way. I suppose, if she insists on pursuing such a pointless (and dangerous!) pastime, I can applaud her for learning something each time she falls, since that's a lesson that can benefit each one of us in various ways. But when I was taking my first spiritual baby steps, I had yet to meet Ginny or hear about any of her skiing adventures, so the term *face-plant* was not yet in my vocabulary—though its meaning would soon be permanently imprinted in my memory bank.

Just like a real toddler, as a spiritual toddler I was determined to mature quickly, to try anything, even if I fell in the process. I decided that if I did fall I would simply jump right back up and declare, "When I fall, I will arise," and be on my way again. Unfortunately determination isn't always enough to prevent face-plants.

It all started when I heard about the women's retreat. I'd never been on a retreat before, but it wasn't hard to imagine how wonderful it must be. Our pastor's wife stood before the congregation every Sunday morning for six weeks and encouraged us to sign up. Then she'd introduce someone who attended the previous year's retreat, and that woman would tell of the amazing spiritual transformation that had taken place in her life during that glorious two-day period. By the end of the six-week promotional routine, all but the most spiritually bankrupt among us were counting the days.

Friday afternoon finally arrived, and I squeezed into the backseat of Laurie's VW Bug. A former hippie who'd become a Christian a few years earlier, Laurie was still driving the car that had been her trademark throughout her anti-everything days. The old VW was covered with faded flowers and peace signs, and it was nearly impossible to decipher its original color. More than once I asked Laurie why she didn't at least repaint her "doodlebug," as she called it, but she insisted its exterior served as a reminder—to herself and others—of what Jesus had done for her. Still, sharing the backseat with two other ladies and three very large and very full overnight bags, as Laurie and her mother sat comfortably in the front, I couldn't help but wish I'd insisted on taking my car, even if it was a gas hog and the mid-'70s gas crunch was in full swing. I'd tried to explain that the five of us would be much more comfortable in my ancient but roomy Buick, but Laurie argued that we didn't want to waste time waiting in gas lines to fill up my monstrosity when we could be there in half the time with her never-needs-gas, flower-child doodlebug. She had a point, so I decided to make the best of it. It was only a two-hour drive, and I certainly didn't want to give anyone at the retreat the impression that I was spiritually immature by arriving in a grouchy or ungrateful mood. As it turned out, no one even noticed my mood by the time we got there. They were too busy trying to help me unfold my left leg so I could "deplane" from Laurie's torture chamber. (I made a mental note to launch a search for an alternate ride home.)

As I hobbled to the welcome center to get my room assignment and pick up the schedule of events, I couldn't help but notice the wide variety of wardrobe styles. The retreat flyer had stressed casual dress, and I thought I had packed accordingly. My fellow doodlebug passengers (with the exception of Laurie's mother, who was in her late forties and therefore excused from knowing or caring about current fashion trends, which explained her brown polyester pantsuit and equally brown loafers) had obviously interpreted "casual dress" the same way I had—relatively clean jeans without holes, and T-shirts and tennis shoes to match. If they wanted pantsuits and loafers they should have specified "formal" and restricted the retreat to those who were old enough to actually own and be willing to be seen in polyester.

I soon decided that "casual dress" meant different things to different people because quite a few women were wearing skirts and high heels. I owned a couple of skirts and occasionally wore them to church on Sunday mornings, but I certainly didn't consider them "casual." And the one time I dared try on a pair of high heels, I decided they'd been invented by the devil. But at least I'd had the good sense not to bring along any of my leftover '60s tie-dye shirts!

As I studied the retreat schedule on the way to my room, I was surprised at the number of meetings and worship services that had been crammed into the 48-hour period, as I'd expected more "communing with God and nature" time. But maturity requires discipline, I reminded myself, as I arrived at my room and fitted the key into the lock, so in my quest for maturity I would make it a point to attend every one of those meetings and services.

Imagine my surprise when I walked into the room and discovered three ladies I'd never met before, all in various stages of dressing or undressing. I'm not sure what shocked me more—their complete lack of modesty or the fact that I didn't know any of them. I understood there would be women from other churches attending the retreat, but I guess it never occurred to me that my roommates would all be strangers—nearly naked strangers at that.

They were all quite friendly, however, and though we ranged in age from an engaged-to-be-married 20-year-old to a 60-year-old grandmother who said she was thankful for everything, including the fact that she still had most her teeth, we were soon chatting as if we'd known each other our whole lives. Things seemed to progress smoothly, and as we returned to our room after the opening meet-and-greet service that evening, I congratulated myself on how well I was fitting in.

Then it was time to go to bed. The 20-year-old and the 60-year-old quickly settled in together on one of the queen-sized beds. "Good night," they called out in unison, and promptly fell asleep.

That left me—and Marcy.

My Leaky Roommate

"Which side do you want?" Marcy asked, a warm smile on her chubby but pleasant face, as she hovered over the remaining bed.

I returned her smile, thinking that it made little difference, as Marcy easily outweighed me by fifty pounds, so the chances that I'd actually get an entire "side" of the bed were definitely not good. Before I could respond, she added, "I suppose I should warn you—I snore. At least, that's what my husband tells me."

My smile was fading fast. "No problem. I'm a sound sleeper, so I doubt I'll even hear you." I excused myself to go brush my teeth (and to ask God to forgive me for lying). By the time I returned Marcy had sprawled out on the right side of the bed and was sawing logs like a beaver on steroids. At least I didn't have to worry about which side of the bed to choose.

I turned off the one remaining light, climbed in on the left side of the bed, and hung on. It was going to be a long night.

I must have finally dozed off some time in the predawn hours, because when the alarm woke me at six I'd been dreaming that I was drowning. Sure enough, my right shoulder was lying on a very large wet spot on the sheet.

"Sorry," Marcy apologized. "I forgot to tell you—I leak." She laughed at my look of confusion and explained, "I'm nursing. Actually, I've just about got Melinda weaned, but... well, you understand."

"Sure," I said, nodding weakly and wondering how fast I'd have to run to get first dibs on the shower. Then I wondered how I'd be able to think of anything else all day other than the fact that I still had one more night to share a bed with Marcy.

Amazingly, bleary-eyed and fuzzy-brained as I was, I actually found myself focusing on the speakers and even taking notes as the day progressed. By the evening service I had gotten a second wind, and when we broke up into groups, I realized I was laughing and having a great time, admittedly thankful that I hadn't ended up in the group next to mine, which had Marcy as its leader. There was only so much togetherness I could handle with my noisy, leaky bunkmate.

Discussion within the groups centered on what we believed God had been speaking to us during the first 24 hours of the retreat. With nearly 20 groups of 10 women each, the noise level in the room soon reached previously unrecorded decibel levels. I strained to hear what the others in my group were sharing, much of which had to do with adapting to the different personalities of their roommates and how God was using those differences to reveal their own weaknesses and idiosyncrasies.

I was pleasantly surprised to discover I wasn't the only one having a hard time adapting to previously unknown and somewhat annoying or eccentric roommates. But I had to admit this was the first time I'd entertained the thought that maybe God wanted me to learn something from the experience. All I had to do was figure out what it might be so I'd have something to say when it was my turn.

I fretted as the discussion edged its way around the circle in my direction. I had to say something, and it had to be spiritual—and humble—or they'd all know I was a fraud, that I wasn't spiritually mature at all. Whatever had given me the idea that I'd graduated from crawling to walking? I had nothing to offer, nothing to contribute to the discussion. Why had I even come to this retreat? I should have stayed home where I belonged.

It was my turn. I opened my mouth, but nothing came out. I considered just moving my lips and hoping the others would think I was saying something wise and mature, and that they couldn't hear me because of all the noise in the room. But the group was leaning toward me expectantly, waiting....

I cleared my throat. Maybe, if I started talking, God would help me out and give me something to say so I wouldn't look like a complete fool. "I..."

"Speak up, dear," one of the older ladies begged, cupping her hand over her ear. "I don't hear very well."

I sat up straighter and cleared my throat again. *Help me, God, I prayed silently.* I began to recount my experiences from the time I opened the door to my room the day before.

The ladies chuckled and nodded knowingly as I told of my surprise at meeting three women I didn't know, all of them changing clothes and chattering like magpies. *Come on, God, help me out here,* I prayed, a bit more desperately this time, as I closed in on the end of my story and still had no idea how to tie it all together with what God was showing or speaking to me—since up till now He didn't seem to be showing or speaking anything.

I could feel the beads of sweat on my forehead as I wrapped up my story with the account of waking up on a wet sheet. Apparently I had been so intent on listening for God to give me something to say that I hadn't heard the conference leader call us to attention. As I launched into my final sentence, all conversation but mine stopped, and I declared at the top of my lungs, "That's when Marcy told me she leaked."

It was one of those moments when you wish you could be set on fire and become an instant martyr for Christ, because that's the only thing that could salvage your reputation. As my cheeks flamed and I wondered if God had seen fit to allow me to spontaneously combust, I heard someone laugh. It was Marcy.

All eyes quickly diverted from me to my leaky roommate, as Marcy stood up and looked around the room, her eyes dancing as she explained my comment to everyone present. By the time she finished, everyone was laughing. I tried to join in, hoping to redeem at least a shred of my dignity, though I doubted it would work.

As Marcy sat down, the conference leader spoke into her microphone. "What a great story," she said, still chuckling. "And you know something? I think God has a message in it for all of us."

I was stunned. What could God possibly have to say to all of us as a result of my humiliating gaffe?

"We all leak," the conference leader announced, as a hush fell over the room. "Or, at least, we should. We need to spend so much time in God's presence that we literally overflow with His Spirit—leak, if you will—onto everyone we meet. Then, once we've leaked God's love onto others, we need to get right back into His presence and get filled up again.

"Ladies, God didn't redeem us just so we could die and go to heaven some day. He wants us to impact people with His love, wherever we go and whatever we do, because there's a hurting world out there that needs Jesus as much as we do. We have no right to keep Him to ourselves. We need to stay so full of God's Spirit and His love that we leak all over everyone we meet!"

A gentle laughter rippled through the room, as heads nodded in agreement, but my face still burned in shame. Thanks to the spiritual maturity of my leaky roommate and a very discerning conference leader, my embarrassing comment had taken a backseat to what God was speaking to us as believers.

But maybe I hadn't come as far from my rug rat days as I thought. I decided this learning-to-walk phase was going to be a lot tougher than I'd expected. I'd just experienced my first spiritual face-plant—but it certainly wouldn't be my last.

 **Making It Personal**

We've all experienced embarrassing moments. Years later, we can usually laugh about those times. When you think of experiences like that in your own life, what do you think has changed inside of you that enables you to view those events in a different light?

● ● ● ● ●

To know the love of Christ which passes knowledge; that you may be filled with all the fullness of God.
—Ephesians 3:19

"WHO SIGNED ME UP FOR THAT?"

8

L uci is an elementary schoolteacher. When I first met her, she'd been teaching for only a few years, just slightly longer than I'd been a believer. We met at women's Bible study one evening, and it was one of those immediate connections that we knew would deepen with time.

We were right. Over the years, as our friendship developed, I learned a lot from Luci, primarily because, unlike me, she had been born and raised in a Christian home. Her parents were in full-time ministry, and she had met her husband, a successful Christian businessman, while they were attending Bible college. At the time it seemed we had absolutely nothing in common except our age, our children's ages, and the fact that we both loved Jesus. She, of course, had loved Him for as long as she could remember and couldn't imagine what it would be like to live any other way. I, on the other hand, was just now learning much of what she had absorbed as a child.

One of my first thoughts as I got to know Luci was that her mother would be an excellent candidate for my Proverbs 31 role model, but when Luci told me her mother had suffered a stroke a few years earlier and never recovered, I crossed another possibility off my list. *Too bad Luci isn't a little older. She'd be the perfect role model.* But we were the same age, so I'd just have to keep looking.

One day, just before school resumed in September, we were chatting about my ongoing volunteer work at the preschool, when Luci said, "I wish we could get more parents to volunteer. It seems preschool moms recognize the importance of being involved in their children's early education, but it's nearly impossible to find parents to donate a couple hours a week at the elementary level."

I cringed, as I realized I'd been thinking exactly the same way. Cautiously I asked Luci what would be involved in volunteering a couple of hours a week for the first-grade-and-above crowd.

She laughed. "Nothing to it, especially when you consider you're already doing your part with the preschoolers, which I personally think is more difficult. Why don't you come by my classroom when school starts next week and you can observe for an hour or so?"

The only day I was free to do that was the very first day of school. Chris was spending the day with my parents, so I made arrangements with Luci to drop by her classroom an hour or so before lunch.

When I arrived, I checked in at the office, donned my approved-visitor badge, and made my way to room 7, where Luci valiantly shepherded her flock of 27 first-graders. Now, first-graders may seem young to some people, but I was used to working with the two- to four-year-olds, so these kids seemed pretty grown up to me, even if most of them were a bit anxious about the first day of school.

Luci introduced me to the class and then showed me to a seat at the back of the room. I was impressed with how well behaved the children were, though some did seem to be getting a bit restless as the clock inched its way toward lunchtime.

When the buzzer sounded, Luci instructed the children to form two lines at the doorway, and I got out of my seat to help her herd them into place. We'd nearly succeeded in getting them all in line when we noticed one little boy standing by his desk, gathering his backpack and jacket and looking like he intended to leave for the day.

Luci walked over to him and bent down to make eye contact. "You won't need all those things for lunch, Timmy. You can leave them here for now."

Timmy looked puzzled. "But I always take my backpack and jacket with me when I go home."

Luci smiled. "That was last year when you were in kindergarten. Now you're in first grade, and you don't go home for lunch anymore. You eat lunch in the cafeteria with the other children, and then you come back here to the classroom for a few more hours before you go home for the day."

Timmy's look quickly escalated from puzzled to stunned. Then he dropped his jacket and backpack, put his hands on his hips, and glared as he asked, "Who signed me up for that?"

I could tell Luci was having as difficult a time as I not to burst out laughing, but we managed to control ourselves as Luci said, "It's just the way things are, Timmy. When you finish kindergarten and start first grade, you come to school for the entire day." She smiled as she rose back to her full height, Timmy's eyes following her the whole time. "You'll get used to it. Before you know it, you'll be glad you get to stay longer. Besides, it means you're growing up and becoming one of the big kids now."

Timmy's indignant look melted to guarded optimism as he slowly made his way to the front of the room to join his classmates. Luci and I exchanged a smile and a wink, and followed them out the door.

It's a Start

"What do you think?" Luci asked when we had a few spare minutes during the lunch break.

I grinned. "I have to admit, other than Timmy wanting to know who signed him up to hang around here all day, it really does look easier than what I'm doing at the preschool—fewer loose cannons rolling around, if you know what I mean."

Luci laughed. "So what are you going to do about it?"

I shrugged. "I'm not sure yet. I'm already committed to volunteering a few hours a week during Chris's last year of preschool, but it was nice being in a classroom where the kids actually sit at desks and pay attention to what's going on."

Luci laughed again. "Obviously you haven't been here for an entire day yet, but it's a start."

I agreed; it was indeed a start, and we'd see what came of it. Meanwhile, I had to pick up Chris and race home in time to throw in some laundry and get dinner started before the rest of the gang showed up and started making their "where's-the-food?" noises.

By the time I'd left my parents' house with my youngest son in tow, I'd promised to take my dad to his doctor's appointment at the VA (Veterans Affairs) the next day, and I'd also realized that Chris hadn't taken a nap and was therefore not in one of his better moods. As he whined all the way home, my head ached in time with the rise and fall of his complaints. He didn't want to leave Grandma and Grandpa's and hated what I was fixing for dinner; he wanted to stay and have what Grandma was fixing; he didn't want to take a bath before he went to bed; he didn't think it was fair that he had to go to bed earlier than everyone else (at that point, it was probably his best chance at not getting a sock stuffed in his mouth before morning).

Miraculously we all survived the night, but the next day wasn't much better. I'd forgotten that a trip to the VA with my dad was an all-day event—and an interesting one at that. Dad was never one to wait patiently or quietly anywhere, for anything or anyone. The fact that he was nearly deaf and refused to wear a hearing aid may have had something to do with it, as he tended to speak very loudly to compensate for not being able to hear. Consequently, questions like, "Do you have anything in your purse for gas?" or "Aren't you a little young to be getting a pot belly?" echoed off the walls and reverberated off my nerve endings as I reminded myself that next time it was my brother's turn to take Dad to the doctor.

To compound the problem, we had Chris with us, who spent the majority of the day running in circles, while my dad handed him pieces of candy in a vain attempt to get him to sit down for more than seven seconds at a time, all the while asking me at the top of his lungs what was wrong with my son.

"Kids today just don't know how to behave," he announced, as he handed Chris yet another piece of candy. "You really ought to learn how to control him better."

I gritted my teeth and snagged Chris by the belt loop as he sailed past me for the umpteenth time. "Sit...down... now," I hissed, donning what was known around my house as "Mom's crazy face." Chris blinked as he recognized the look, and then reluctantly sat down next to me, where he remained for nearly a full minute. By the time the receptionist called my dad's name, I was ready to start running around the room behind my son, hoping that someone might snag me and pop me into a padded cell for a couple of hours where I could have some peace and quiet.

We finally made it back to my parents' house, where Chris repeated his "I don't want to eat your crummy food; I just want to stay with Grandma and Grandpa" routine— all the way out their door and into the car, throughout the drive home, and right up until he dropped off to sleep in the middle of his "I don't know why I have to go to bed before everybody else" mantra.

As I fell into bed that night, enjoying the quiet of a sleeping household, I remembered that the next day was my volunteer day at the preschool, and I almost laughed out loud when the thought popped into my mind: *Who signed me up for that?*

It seemed six-year-old Timmy and I had a lot more in common than I'd realized. It didn't help much to reflect on the truth of Luci's words that all this was just part of growing up and being one of the "big kids now." As much as I hated to admit it, I sometimes missed being one of the little kids— one of those loose cannons who could dismiss responsibility and devote my time and energy to playing and having fun.

I sighed, closing my eyes as sleep called my name. In a matter of minutes I drifted off to the thought that maybe tomorrow I'd manage to find a little time to look for my Proverbs 31 role model.

 Making It Personal

Think of the times in your life when you've felt pulled in so many directions that you wondered who signed you up for such an assignment. How did your relationship with the Lord affect your attitude? Were you able to turn the situation over to Him? If not, why? What can you do differently now when you feel caught in such demanding situations?

With goodwill doing service, as to the Lord, and not to men, knowing that whatever good anyone does, he will receive the same from the Lord, whether he is a slave or free.
—Ephesians 6:7–8

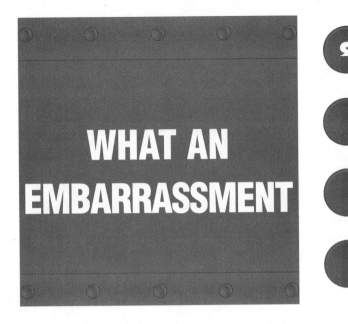

WHAT AN EMBARRASSMENT

9

As Chris progressed through his final year of preschool and into kindergarten, my older sons, Al and Mike, were entering that preteen stage where they suddenly questioned the things they once accepted on blind faith—things like their parents' ability to walk on water or, for that matter, to do anything other than embarrass their children simply by existing. I naively believed that spending a little quality time with them would remedy the problem.

One of the first things I did was take all three boys swimming. They hadn't been in the pool more than five minutes when the two older ones decided to use their younger brother as a beach ball. I immediately tried to intervene—not so much because I was concerned with Chris's welfare but because there was a very large sign posted beside the pool stating, "No pool toys allowed." I wasn't absolutely sure, but I had a strong suspicion that my youngest qualified as a pool toy at that point. However, all my shrieking and arm waving did no good whatsoever, as Al and Mike continued to toss their completely happy and cooperative little brother back and forth between them.

I finally had to jump into the water to get their attention—not something I had anticipated doing. Having just that morning washed and styled my hair, I was perfectly content to lie in the sun and read, peeking up occasionally to make sure all was well. There were countless other people at the pool, so I didn't really think my three water-lovers-who-swim-like-fish needed my constant supervision. Obviously, I was wrong.

Making my way through a throng of swimmers who, for the most part, had stopped to watch my three geniuses and to place bets on which of the two older ones would drop their beach-ball brother first, I finally managed to get close enough to get their attention. Both of them, forgetting they even had a little brother, stared at me in horror, as if I'd just flown in from another planet with the sole purpose of ruining their lives.

Al recovered first. "Mom's in the water," he stated, in a tone one would expect from someone saying, "Mom has two heads." Mike nodded in response, too shocked to speak. Chris bobbed up from the bottom of the pool and broke the surface just in time to notice the drama unfolding among his wet family. Wisely, he quickly dove back under and darted away, leaving his older brothers to wish they could do the same.

It wasn't that they were afraid of me—it was simply that their lives were over. It's one thing to have your mom surreptitiously overseeing your activities from the side of the pool, but to have her actually get in the water and talk to you was social suicide. The worst part of the entire incident happened as we headed home later that day and I overheard the three of them discussing the humiliating incident.

"How embarrassing," Al groaned.

"I'll never come back to this pool again," Mike declared.

Chris—the one I had jumped into the pool to rescue as he sailed through the air—chimed in, "Yeah, and we were having so much fun—until Mom got in the water."

You'd think I'd learn, wouldn't you?

Not me. (Remember, I still hadn't found my Proverbs 31 role model, so I was operating on my own. Scary thought!) A few days later I happened to walk outside and discovered the older members of the socially devastated trio practicing turns and swerves on their skateboards. I watched for a while, marveling at how quickly they had grown from those adorable little rug rats who spent the majority of their time crying, sleeping, and spitting up. I'd even noticed that they were beginning to consider girls to be acceptable and possibly even desirable life forms, though the female species hadn't quite caught up with football and motorcycles on their favorites list.

When Mike zoomed past and noticed me, he nodded his head almost imperceptibly—the standard display of acknowledgment from one who wished to appear cool at all times. Another minute or two passed, and by now both sons were aware of my presence and the fact that I was observing them. When they realized that ignoring me wasn't making me go away, they rolled to a stop in front of me.

"Something wrong, Mom?" Al asked.

"Nope. Just watching my handsome sons display their talent."

They rolled their eyes in unison.

"Sooo...do you need something?" Mike asked.

I shrugged. "Nope. Like I said, just watching."

They were studying me now, no doubt checking for an ulterior motive. Suddenly Al's eyes lit up with one of his "I've got a great idea" looks—which should have been a dead giveaway that it was anything *but* a great idea.

"Hey, Mom," he said, getting off his board and picking it up, "you want to ride? You used to ride when you were a kid, right?"

Now we're *really* talking ancient history. The skateboard I used to ride was literally a *skate-board*—a board with the four wheels from my roller skates attached to the bottom.

And it had been years—decades, actually. But how hard could it be? People don't forget how to ride a bike. Wouldn't riding a skateboard be the same?

A Padded Seat

"Sure, why not?" I said, taking the board from his outstretched hands, as he and his brother looked from me to each other and back again, their eyes wide with surprise and anticipation. Could this be their chance for revenge on the swimming pool incident?

I set the board down on the slightly sloping driveway and jumped on. My ride lasted less than a second, as the board went out from under me and flew into the street, while my wide-glide rear end crash-landed on the cement. It was the first and only time I can remember being glad for those extra ten pounds.

"Mom, are you all right?" they both asked, lifting me from the driveway.

"I'm fine," I insisted, brushing myself off and trying to blink the stars from my eyes and the ringing from my ears. I really wasn't fine, but I imagined I would be in a week or so. And I wasn't about to tell them otherwise.

I appreciated their solicitous care as they escorted me into the house, and I'm not saying they weren't sincere in their concern, but there was an inordinate amount of laughter on their part throughout the rest of the day—except when I came into view. Then they quickly got serious and asked again if I was OK.

I suppose I was. I had no broken bones or serious bruises, but I haven't stepped on a skateboard since—nor do I intend to. Skateboards have come to symbolize a Scripture that I came across the very next morning as I was reading through a couple of chapters in 1 Corinthians: *"Therefore let him who thinks he stands take heed lest he fall"* (10:12). It seemed I'd been spending a lot of time doing spiritual face-plants lately, and I was beginning to feel more than a bit discouraged.

Why hadn't I found a role model to help me in my quest to become like the Proverbs 31 woman? Surely there was someone out there who not only qualified to be my mentor, but who was also willing and available to do so. What was the holdup?

A few days later I was lamenting the situation to my mom, leaving out the part about the skateboard incident. Mom already thought I took far too many risks and should settle down and accept that I was getting older and live accordingly. (Oh, sure. And I could just go out and buy a polyester pantsuit while I was at it, and then I'd fit right in!)

"Do you think maybe you're being too picky?" Mom asked.

"Picky?" I frowned. "No, I don't think so. After all, you can't just have anybody for a role model. Mom, you and I didn't grow up in Christian homes. We need somebody who did and who's been a Christian for a long time and has her life and family in order. There must be somebody out there like that—somewhere."

Mom shrugged. "If you say so. But what are you going to do to find her? Take out an ad? Put up a sign?"

Poor Mom. She tried to be funny, but it didn't work. The thought flashed through my mind that my children probably thought the same thing about me, but I dismissed it as quickly as it came. "I'll keep praying and looking. I know God's going to bring her along sometime. I guess I just have to be patient."

Mom smiled. "Do you think you can do that?"

I knew what she was thinking. Patience hadn't exactly been my strong point in life. "I don't really have a choice, do I?" I got up from the kitchen table, ready to head home.

"Are you OK?" Mom asked. "You look like you're limping a bit."

I wasn't about to tell her my built-in seat cushion was bruised, so I smiled and assured her I was fine, as I walked out the door and headed for my car.

Once I was settled into the driver's seat, Mom leaned down and peered into the open window. "Keep looking," she said, doing what she did best—being an encouraging mother. "I'm sure that spiritual superwoman mentor will turn up soon."

I nodded and sighed. "I know you're right. And thanks for saying so. Meanwhile, I'll just keep praying and doing the best I can."

Mom smiled as I started the engine. "That's all any of us can do. Remember what the Bible says in Jeremiah, that God's plans for you are good. That includes helping you mature into the godly woman He planned for you to become long before you were ever born."

I returned Mom's smile. She always seemed to know the right thing to say. It's too bad she hadn't been a Christian long enough to be my role model.

Making It Personal

What incidents in your life bring to mind the verse in 1 Corinthians: *"Therefore let him who thinks he stands beware lest he fall"* (10:12)? How did those incidents give opportunity to others to speak wisdom into your life and to help you see situations from God's limitless point of view, rather than your own limited one? Can you think of someone who may be in need of hearing similar words from you today?

For I know the thoughts that I think toward you, says the Lord, thoughts of peace and not of evil, to give you a future and a hope.
—Jeremiah 29:11

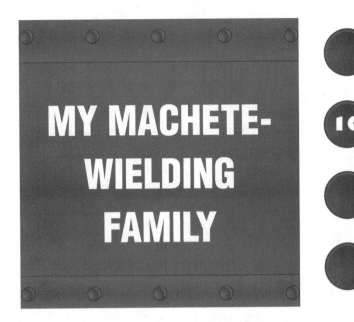

MY MACHETE-WIELDING FAMILY

10

I wanted to believe I was through embarrassing my children (so did they!), but it would be awhile yet before they were old enough to approve being seen with me in public again. In the meantime I had resolved not to set myself up anymore. From now on I'd leave the skateboarding and other questionable pursuits to the experts and concentrate on finding that spiritual superwoman who continued to elude me.

So what made me think I'd find her on a Christmas tree farm? Yet there I was, slogging through the Washington State rain and mud during the season known affectionately as the "rain festival," which lasts from October to May, helping my retired dad trim trees before the buyers showed up to place their orders. It was only mid-November, but the Hawaii buyers wanted theirs before Thanksgiving, since the trees had to travel all the way to Aloha-land on ships. Dad thought he could save some money if the whole machete-wielding family pitched in and walked the ten acres of spruce and fir and various other evergreens, swinging and hacking and praying we'd still have all our limbs and digits by the end of the day. Otherwise, he would have to pay professionals who knew what they were doing and could get it done in a tenth of the time; in his mind, that was not an option.

"There's nothing to it," he explained. "All you have to do is shape them a little. The buyers will send someone to cut them and haul them away. When we're done, we'll take the money we saved and go out to eat." (Can someone say "McBurger Deluxe"?)

I don't mean to imply that my dad was tight, but he was born and raised in Germany during the World War I era. He watched his baby brother die as a result of malnutrition, while he himself spent time in a government-run hospital, suffering from scurvy. When he arrived in the United States at the ripe old age of 18, alone and basically destitute, it was 1929—just in time for the Depression. As a result Dad knew what it was like to work hard and seldom have enough of anything. He never got over that mind-set, and he did his best to drill it into his kids. It must have worked because to this day I still hang paper towels to dry in the sun and recycle rubber bands left over from when my brother was a paperboy in the early 1960s.

So there we were, all the kids and grandkids who were old enough to walk in the mud and swing a sickle at the same time, making our way up one row of trees and down the next, swinging and slicing and praying for the best. I never was sure if we helped or hindered the shaping process, but Dad was happy with the cheap labor, and by the end of a miserable day, even greasy hamburgers and fries tasted good.

As we sat there munching away, my nephew Larson asked, "Aunt Kathi, why did Grandpa buy a Christmas tree farm?"

We were all wondering the same thing at that point—not to mention wondering why we had let ourselves get roped into "helping"—but I knew farm living had been my dad's lifelong dream. When he retired in his 60s, after working for decades at a job he hated just so he could support his family, Dad left crowded Southern California behind and headed for the Pacific Northwest, with my mom tied to the back of the truck and dragging her heels all the way. Moving from the land of sunshine and surf to the rain capital of the world was not her idea of a step up. But my parents were part of America's "greatest generation"—the ones who worked hard, won wars, and stayed married. So here we were—we kids having grown up and migrated north to be near our parents' new nest.

Now my dad's farm hadn't originally been a Christmas tree farm. When he first bought it, he planned to raise cows. Then someone suggested he might want to have a horse or two, since he had plenty of room. Dad looked at him as if he'd suggested my father jump from the roof, flap his arms, and fly.

"Are you crazy? You can't eat horses. What good are they? They destroy the pastures, eat the hay, and run the meat off the cows. What would I want with horses?"

So he stuck with cows—which was fine with us until it was time to butcher one of them. No, I'm not a whimpering animal lover who grew attached to old Bessie and couldn't handle the thought of eating her. I'll take a grilled steak over a head of lettuce any day, regardless of the source. The part I hated was the actual butchering, cutting, and wrapping process.

This was another one of Dad's surefire ways to save money by having us do all the work. He and a couple of his buddies would kill the cow and then take it into my dad's huge workshop, where they'd use his electric table saw to cut the meat. Then they'd bring it inside the house for the rest of us to wrap and label. Wrapping wasn't so hard, but labeling was a challenge because Dad had no experience or training as a butcher. He had a meat chart on the wall of his shop and tried to match the cuts to the chart, but we were never sure if we were wrapping a shoulder roast or a T-bone steak. The only thing we recognized clearly was the hamburger, as we got to help with that. Dad would plop down a huge tray of meat chunks and say, "Grind it up." That's where my squeamish stomach kicked in.

Somehow we got through it, though it was always an adventure to pull a package of meat from the freezer and try to figure out what part of Old Bessie it really was. That leads me to the reason we didn't mind so much slogging through the mud and trees and swinging a machete in the rain....

When Dad decided the cows weren't paying off like he'd expected and opted to invest in seedlings and start growing Christmas trees, we were ecstatic. Trees were nonmobile and required a lot less work than their mooing predecessors. That was the story I told Larson in response to his question about why Grandpa had a Christmas tree farm—and why helping him trim the trees wasn't all that bad.

His face paled a bit as I mentioned the butchering and hamburger grinding, though he admitted it wouldn't have deterred him in his passion for eating meat. Still, it did seem to make him appreciate the seemingly endless rows of yuletide greenery we'd worked on all day.

If You Think of It That Way

"So you see," I concluded, "trimming trees isn't such a bad job."

He shrugged. "I guess not."

"Too bad you can't help on Monday," I commented.

His eyes lit up. "That's right. I have to go to school, so I can't work in the trees."

I grinned at the sound of excitement in his voice. It does an aunt's heart good to see her nephew so enamored at the thought of studying compound fractions and the War of 1812.

"So what about the Christmas trees?" he asked. "Whose idea was that?"

I frowned. Hadn't he been paying attention? "It was your grandpa's. When he got tired of all the work involved with the cows—"

"That's not what I meant," Larson interrupted. "I was just wondering where the idea of Christmas trees got started, and what do they have to do with Jesus?"

He had me on that one. I'd been a Christian long enough to know that some believers observed only the religious aspects of the holiday, while others went all out with decorations and trees and Santa and reindeer and elves. I felt a bit caught in the middle. I didn't care for the commercialized aspects of Christmas, and I thought it was sad that so many celebrated the occasion without giving even a thought to the One whose birth brought salvation to the world. But how did I really feel about all the hoopla that went with the holiday? If I thought the merchandising hoopla and removal of Christ from Christmas was wrong, where did I draw the line? Should I stop baking Christmas cookies? What about gifts and decorating? What about the trees we trimmed today and from which my dad supplemented his retirement income?

My young nephew, sitting across from me and dipping fries into a large mound of soppy ketchup, had stirred up some serious concerns in my heart. I hadn't even been able to track down a Proverbs 31 role model, and now I had another dilemma.

About the time I'd decided Larson had long since forgotten our topic of conversation, he said, "I don't know if this is the reason we have Christmas trees or not, but doesn't the Bible say something about Jesus hanging on a tree? The cross was made of wood, right? Maybe Christmas trees could be a reminder of what He did for us—if we want to think of it that way."

He shrugged and went back to eating, as his words echoed in my mind: *If we want to think of it that way.* That was the answer, wasn't it? We can choose to think of the Christmas tree as something to hang a bunch of decorations on and put presents under, or we can choose to think of it as a reminder of what Jesus did for us. We can choose to think of the gifts under the tree as more material possessions, or we can choose to think of them as reminders of the gifts the Magi brought to honor the toddler King. We can choose to think of the season as a time of lengthy to-do lists and errands and appointments, or we can choose to think of it as a time to get together with our friends and loved ones and worship God as we pass along the story of the Savior born in a manger.

Whether it is Christmas or Easter or the Fourth of July, shopping or working or eating, weddings or funerals or picnics, health or illness, birth or death—whatever comes into our lives each day presents us with a choice. We can choose to deal with these occasions and situations in ways that serve and honor only ourselves, or we can choose to deal with them in ways that honor the God we claim to serve.

For some inexplicable reason, as I sat in that fast-food restaurant with my nephew and the rest of the family after a long, hard day of slicing and dicing my dad's Christmas trees, I smiled as I felt my heart warm with the knowledge that somehow I was getting closer to my goal of becoming a Proverbs 31 woman. I wasn't exactly sure what my nephew's insights had contributed to that assurance, but I was relatively certain they were somehow connected.

 Making It Personal

What are some of your most unusual memories from family get-togethers? Were there times in the midst of those occasions where you gleaned a nugget of truth from an unlikely source? How has God used those moments from the past to impact your life now? Regarding Larson's comment, how are you choosing to think about circumstances in your life? From God's perspective or yours?

One person esteems one day above another; another esteems every day alike. Let each be fully convinced in his own mind. He who observes the day, observes it to the Lord; and he who does not observe the day, to the Lord he does not observe it.
—Romans 14:5–6

Learning to Run—Swift and Steady, Still on My Feet

Do you not know that in a race all the runners run, but one receives the prize? Run in such a way that you may obtain it.
—1 Corinthians 9:24

I'm Running as Fast as I Can!

Over the years I've probably owned every type of exercise equipment ever made—each guaranteed to make me look younger and better than I did 20 years earlier. I tried the stationary bike, treadmill, handheld weights, exercise videos, and even the dreaded stair-climbing machine, the most torturous contraption ever invented. For the most part each one ended up being turned into a planter or sold at garage sales...except the weights and videos, which are lurking somewhere in the back of my closet. Each time I acquired a new piece of exercise equipment I did so with high hopes and what I thought were even higher commitment levels. During my brief relationship with each wonder-working item, I learned something very important: Regardless of how hard or how fast you run, you can only run in place for so long. Eventually boredom or exhaustion wins out, and you give up. Who wants to exercise to the point of pain (and beyond) while staring at the same four walls? Besides, no one stands on the sidelines to cheer you on in a stationary race. There are no high-fives from adoring fans (or sympathetic supporters) to encourage you along the way. And there is no one to hang a medal around your neck at the end of the event. Running in place offers little or no incentive to keep on keeping on.

I tried all the usual diversions: dragging the treadmill in front of the TV (don't even ask why I didn't pick up the portable TV and place it in front of the treadmill instead); balancing an open book on the handlebars of my stationary bike (vertigo and glasses that slide down my nose when I sweat put an end to that); listening to music while I annihilated my legs climbing stationary stairs (ten minutes into that routine all I could hear was the pounding of blood in my ears, screaming, "You'd better stop NOW if you want to live to see tomorrow!"); and trying to identify with the young, perfectly sculpted female instructors on the videos, none of whom had ever had children or tipped the scales at more than 99 pounds. Needless to say, none of these things worked, and my exercise routines all bit the proverbial dust.

After all this, you'd think I'd learned my lesson, right? I'm afraid not. My friend (and I use the term loosely) Linda convinced me I'd do better—meaning, make more progress and be more consistent—if I went to the gym with her three mornings a week. Against my better judgment, I agreed. The experience was...well, not all I'd hoped for or been led to believe. I was still jumping, climbing, twirling, and running in place, only now I had company—an entire room full of overweight, middle-aged, tutu-clad divas breathing hard, sweating profusely, and going nowhere. And I was paying for the privilege to be a part of it!

Wouldn't you suppose I'd be smart enough to figure out that trying to run in place spiritually, regardless of how many distractions or variations I attempted to incorporate into my routine, wouldn't work either? Nope, not me. I kept tripping over my self—as in me, myself, and I. Every time the thought flitted through my mind that maybe I wasn't quite as far along in my personal spiritual race as I thought, I quickly dismissed that pesky notion and redoubled my efforts. Just work harder, I told myself. I was determined to finish the race, to finish it well, and to finish it first—all amidst the sound of cheering angels and a colorful rain of celestial confetti. I was sure my "tight ship" was right around the corner, and loose cannons would soon be a thing of the past.

I had outgrown the rug rat and toddler stages, but I still had a lot to learn about the difference between a sprinter and a marathon runner, particularly if I ever hoped to achieve the Proverbs 31 status that beckoned me forward....

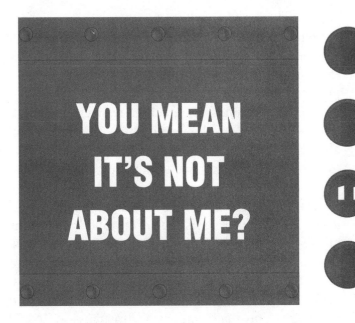

YOU MEAN IT'S NOT ABOUT ME?

Though I'd experienced more than a few disappointments and disillusionments—not to mention some loose cannons spinning wildly on deck—along the way, I was glad to be past the rug rat and toddler stages of my spiritual life. Maturity had exacted its price, but it felt good to know I had finally achieved stability as a believer. I could now step out in faith—and confidence—and find my place of ministry in the body of Christ. No longer a baby Christian, I was now a bona fide disciple, ready to teach and lead others to spiritual maturity.

Imagine my surprise when I asked about teaching one of the Sunday morning adult Bible classes, only to have the pastor advise me to take some ministry training courses first.

"The classes are held here at the church every Monday evening," he explained. "There's a bit of homework involved, but nothing major—just enough to help equip you for the responsibilities of being in leadership."

He must have noticed my shocked expression, because he quickly added, "That doesn't mean you can't get involved in ministry in the meantime. While you're taking the classes, we encourage you to volunteer in some area of church service, sort of in an 'apprentice' capacity. If teaching is what you feel drawn to, maybe you can assist the current adult Bible class teachers for a semester or two."

Assist the adult Bible class teachers? What was he talking about? I'd volunteered as an aide in the children's classes before, but I couldn't imagine that he meant for me to bring crackers and juice to the adult classes, or help pass out crayons, or...

Wait a minute. Now that I thought about it, I had seen a couple of people assisting in the Sunday morning adult classes from time to time—helping to prepare the classrooms, running off copies of lesson sheets, writing prayer requests or scripture references on the chalkboard. Is that what he meant? Is that why I'd spent the last few years of my life learning to crawl and walk as a Christian—so I could make copies and set up chairs? Was he serious?

One look at my pastor's eyes and I knew he was. OK, if taking classes on Monday nights and setting up chairs on Sunday mornings was what it took to move into the ranks of church leadership, then I'd be the best class-taker and chair-setter-upper that church had ever seen! I smiled, nodded, and asked, "Where do I sign up?"

He chuckled. "You don't have to decide right this minute. This is quite an undertaking—and quite a commitment. You might want to take a little time to pray about this first."

I shook my head. "No way. I've already prayed, and I know this is what I want to do. The sooner I get started, the quicker I can get it over with—" I caught myself and swallowed, as heat crept up my neck and into my cheeks. "I mean... I'm... just anxious to get started teaching, and..."

His kind smile made me feel worse. I thought I was through with face-plants, and there I was, doing my best imitation of Peter, the sometimes overeager, foot-in-mouth fisherman-turned-disciple, famous for saying the wrong thing at the wrong time. But he meant well, I reminded myself. And Jesus did commend him once or twice. Maybe, if I tried harder and practiced a bit more patience and self-control, Jesus might find a reason to commend me once in awhile too.

"Sorry," I said. "I guess I ran ahead of myself a little...."

He nodded. "I can certainly relate to that. I'm famous for doing the same thing. But if you're serious about taking the ministry classes, you can stop by the office during the week and pick up the schedule. In the meantime, I'll see if we can get you started as a teacher's assistant on Sunday mornings. Sound good?"

"Sure," I said, my enthusiasm more than slightly dampened. In all honesty, it didn't sound good at all. I'd just committed myself—and directly to my pastor, no less—to attend ministry classes (including homework!) and to help out in adult Sunday school. What was I thinking? I'd already been whining about how busy I was, and now I was signing up to be busier than ever. And yet, hadn't I said I wanted to be a mature Christian, a disciple whose life was given over to helping and serving others? Hadn't I learned that the word disciple means "disciplined one"? I sighed. It seemed I'd painted myself into a spiritual maturity corner, and there was no way out. I was just going to have to learn how to run a little faster.

As it turned out, things weren't nearly as bad as I'd expected. I found I actually enjoyed the classes, and the homework really wasn't all that time-consuming. What really surprised me was that I liked assisting in the classrooms on Sunday mornings—maybe not the setting-up-chairs part so much, but running errands and realizing that I actually was doing something useful and helpful "for the Kingdom," as I'd often heard other Christians say.

I also figured all that running around from one class to another, delivering stacks of freshly copied lesson sheets and making sure there was a steaming hot pot of coffee and a plate of doughnuts in each room, was good for keeping me humble. A mature Christian was known for humility and a willingness to serve, right? In fact, we were studying about that very thing in our Monday evening ministry class—"Servant Leadership" it was titled—and I certainly wanted to put into practice everything I was learning at school.

Questioning God

Then one Sunday morning something strange happened. As I was bustling around from one classroom to another, the teacher in one of the rooms asked if I'd mind making a list on the chalkboard. I shrugged and said, "Sure," happy for the chance to model all I was learning about humility and servant leadership. I grabbed a piece of chalk and tuned in to what the teacher was saying.

"That was a good question, Karen," she said, directing her comment to a lady in the back row. "I appreciate your honesty, and I'm sure we've all had similar questions."

I noticed a few heads nodding in agreement, accompanied by a smattering of "amens," and I found myself wishing I'd been paying attention and caught the woman's question.

"OK," the teacher said. "So we're in agreement that Karen isn't the only one who's run into some tough things in her life and wondered why God allowed them to happen. Without getting into details, let's make a list of some of the things that have happened since we've become Christians and that we've found ourselves questioning God about. Then we'll search the Scriptures and talk about what we've learned from our experiences, and see if we can come up with some explanations."

She turned to me and said, "You can start the list with Karen's question about why God allowed her sister to get cancer."

I nodded, relieved that she'd repeated Karen's concern, and wrote it on the board. As I waited for the next question, I found myself thinking, *I don't blame Karen for questioning God about that. If we are God's children, why would He want us or our loved ones to suffer?*

Then the teacher said, "OK, I'll go next. Years ago, when I was a brand new Christian, my husband left me. I had three children to raise and no job. I must admit, I spent a lot of time questioning God in those days."

Underneath Karen's concern about her sister's cancer I wrote, "Deserted by husband and left to raise children alone." That was another good question.

A man with graying hair, 50 or so, said, "I hate to admit it, but I've been questioning God a lot lately. I've worked at the same job for 30 years, and now that my wife and I are getting close to retirement age, they let me go. We have a little money in savings, but we aren't old enough to get Social Security or Medicare yet. What are we supposed to do about medical expenses and home repairs and the cost of living that seems to go up every day? Everyone tells me to trust God and He'll provide, and in my head I know that's true, but my heart isn't so sure."

I added another tough life situation to the growing list. *God never said everything would be easy*, I reminded myself. *Maybe these are all opportunities to grow in our faith. Maybe...* Yet I felt a lot like the man who'd lost his job. I knew in my mind these things were true, but I also knew my heart would have a hard time accepting them if I were the one walking through these trials.

I turned back to the class just in time to see a young woman lift her hand. I'd seen her around the church before and knew she had some disabilities, but I'd never heard her say anything, as she usually stood quietly between her parents and let them do all the talking. From the looks of the others in the classroom, they were as surprised as I to see her raise her hand.

"Yes, Mara," the teacher said, her smile warm and encouraging. "Is there something in your life that has caused you to question God?"

Mara nodded and slowly rose from her chair. Everyone waited, as Mara's eyes darted around the room and she clasped her shaking hands in front of her. It was obvious this was difficult for her, and I had no doubt she was about to ask why God had allowed her to be born with so many physical and mental problems.

With great effort Mara opened her mouth and voiced her thoughts, pausing between words to swallow or take a breath. "I ask God...every day why...He loves me...and why...He's so good to me. I don't...deserve it...but He just...loves me anyway."

Appearing exhausted from the effort, Mara sank back into her chair, her teary-eyed but proud parents flanking her, as the rest of us absorbed her words.

Finally the teacher spoke. "Thank you, Mara. You've helped us put it all back into perspective." She looked around the room, even turning her head to make eye contact with me before saying, "Mara has reminded us all that when we're tempted to question God about something bad that's happened, the question we should be asking is, 'How is it that You could love me so much, God, that You would send Your only Son to die for me?' Sometimes we get so caught up in ourselves we forget how truly amazing grace is."

Her eyes returned to Mara, who sat with her hands folded in her lap. "Thank you again, Mara, for reminding us that it's not about us; it's about Him."

As Mara nodded, I thought, *Isn't that a given? Surely all Christians know it's not about them; it's about Him...don't they? Don't I?*

I turned and replaced the chalk on the ledge below the chalkboard, then picked up the eraser and wiped the board clean, suddenly aware of how very much I still had to learn. Maybe I wasn't running quite as fast as I'd imagined.

Making It Personal

We all have a natural tendency to whine and question God when things don't go as we'd hoped. Consider times when you complained to God about your situation, and then ask yourself how you might have handled things differently if you'd focused on His unconditional and undeserved love for you, rather than on your problem.

In this is love, not that we loved God, but that He loved us and sent His Son to be the propitiation for our sins.
—1 John 4:10

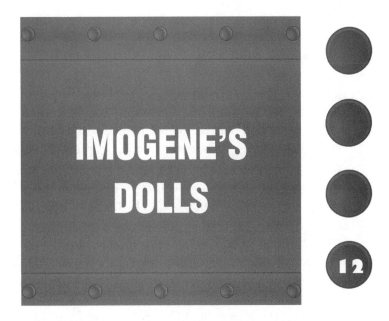

IMOGENE'S DOLLS

12

So it wasn't about me. Now what? And what exactly did "not about me" mean?

It seemed I'd passed through my crawling and walking stages, gaining only more questions and making little or no progress toward finding a Proverbs 31 mentor. The loose cannons were still rolling across my deck, and I was trying not to become discouraged.

Then I ran into Imogene—literally—and it was my fault. If I'd listened to my schoolteacher friend Luci and stuck to volunteering at school, especially now that even my youngest was going there, I wouldn't have gotten it into my head to take a part-time job at the church. It wasn't even the church I attended, mind you, but one a few blocks away, which was looking for a secretary/gopher-type employee for 12 hours a week.

I figured the typing skills I'd learned way back in high school, combined with my grammar skills, would qualify me for the secretary part (this was long before computer knowledge was a mandatory requirement for every job on the market), and the gopher part—well, a housewife and mother was naturally experienced at that sort of thing. Besides, it was only 12 hours a week. How hard could it be?

No one had told me—and I didn't have the sense to ask—why this little church had stayed little for so long. Now don't get me wrong; I like the homey feel of a small church, but I knew enough even then to realize that a healthy church should be growing. This one wasn't. Despite the fact that the neighborhood was exploding with new families moving in, none seemed to be attending this particular church. The only ones who did attend appeared to be the founding fathers and mothers, who'd started the congregation more than 100 years earlier. If they'd had a youth group, it would have consisted of the seven members of the congregation under 65. With an average age in the mid-70s, the church seemed doomed to extinction.

You'd think that would have been a red flag. Why would a dying congregation want to hire a third employee, even part time? They already had a pastor who preached at the Sunday morning service (though I'd heard his messages focused on a social gospel), showed up for most board meetings, and even dropped into the office on occasion on weekdays. They also had a part-time custodian who doubled as a groundskeeper— when he wasn't sneaking off to nap on one of the pews in the sanctuary. But apparently the board had decided they needed someone to come in a few hours a week to answer the phone (which seldom rang), type and print the weekly bulletins, and straighten up the sanctuary on Friday to make sure it was ready for Sunday morning.

As it turned out I got the job by default; no one else applied. That, too, should have been a red flag, but I didn't even notice. I was happy to make a little extra money to help with household expenses without being away from home too many hours to do it. It seemed the perfect job for me, despite my already overloaded schedule, and I accepted without hesitation.

That's when I "ran into" Imogene. It was Friday morning of my first week on the job, as I walked from the office, through the courtyard, and into the hallway that led to the kitchen and all-purpose room in one direction and the sanctuary in the other. I hadn't taken two steps into the hallway before I crashed into a very tall, very broad, and very annoyed mountain of a woman, whose hair was pulled back into a tight silver bun at the nape of her thick neck and whose pale blue eyes shot darts at me as if I'd purposely smacked into her. (Since she was at least twice my size, she should have realized that was highly unlikely, but apparently it didn't even cross her mind.)

"You should watch where you're going," she declared. "You young people have no manners anymore."

I was then in my mid-30s, so being referred to as a young person—even a manner-less one—couldn't be all bad. I forced a smile. "Excuse me. You're right. I should have been paying more attention." I stuck out my right hand and announced, "I'm Kathi, the new secretary. I was just heading for the sanctuary to make sure it's ready for Sunday."

Her hand made no move to grasp mine, and her eyes stayed locked on my face as if I'd just declared my intention to paint the entire building orange. I dropped my hand and waited.

"Secretary," she said, spitting out the word as if it had a bad taste. "I told them we didn't need a secretary. I've been typing the bulletin for 36 years and could do it for another 36, but apparently that wasn't good enough for them."

It seemed I had usurped the job of a woman who planned to live to be at least 120. This could be trouble.

"I didn't realize they had someone else doing my...uh, *your* job before they hired me," I stammered, wondering what else I could say to make the situation worse. It was looking like all I needed to do was open my mouth and I'd automatically find another nail in my coffin.

Imogene's existing look of displeasure was now compounded by scorn. "What do you suppose we did before you showed up? Do you think this church existed for more than a century without a bulletin?"

I hadn't thought about it at all, but somehow I knew that wasn't the answer she wanted to hear. The problem was, I had absolutely no idea what her desired answer might be. I stood there, wondering if I should open my mouth and try to give an appropriate answer, or keep it shut and be satisfied with limiting the damage to its current level.

A Life's Work

Suddenly Imogene's face changed—not that it softened, but the hostility lessened to a slightly less than radioactive reading. "Do you like dolls?" she asked.

How in the world was I supposed to answer a question like that? I hadn't played with dolls in at least 25 years, and to be honest, I wasn't all that crazy about them before that.

I decided I'd better say something, so I took a deep breath and plunged in. "Well, I..."

"Come with me," she said, turning on her heel and marching in the direction of the all-purpose room. I blinked myself back to reality and scurried to keep up. *How could anyone that old move so fast?*

Then she came to a screeching halt, with me right behind her, skidding to a stop just in time to avoid running into her once again. We were just inside the double doors to the all-purpose room, and Imogene reached over to the wall and flipped on the lights. There, in what I could only assume was battle array, were hundreds and hundreds of dolls—big ones, little ones, black ones, white ones, plastic ones, cloth ones, old ones, new ones, male ones, female ones. You get the picture. They were standing and sitting—some on their own, some propped against pillows—on rows and rows of portable shelves, lined up against the wall. In front of them was a lone podium, draped in white lace.

As we stood there, staring, once again I knew I should say something, but once again I didn't have a clue what. I just gaped, waiting and wondering, until Imogene said, "What do you think?"

I gulped. What did I think? That I wish I hadn't taken this job; that I'd applied to help with arts and crafts at the local mental health facility; that I'd signed up for the Green Berets.

I opened my mouth and said, "They're...lovely." I paused before trying again. "Amazing, actually."

Then Imogene did something that truly was amazing—she smiled. She smiled a big, broad, warm, wide smile—a real ear-to-ear, all-the-way-across-her-face smile—and said, "They are, aren't they? And they're all mine."

I raised my eyebrows in surprise, not so much because I was impressed with her remarkable collection, but because I was stunned that anyone could devote his or her entire life to amassing such a menagerie. Had she had time to do anything else, or did these flesh-and-bloodless entities comprise her entire life's work?

I didn't have to wait long for an answer. "I've collected them since I was a child," she said, her voice taking on an almost reverent tone. "I bought some of them new, but others I rescued from thrift stores and even garbage dumps, cleaned them up and made them live again." She looked at me as if she expected me to present her with the Nobel Peace Prize. "Have you ever seen anything like it?"

I swallowed, glad she'd worded her question as she had. "No. Never."

She nodded, satisfied with my response. "I'm giving a talk on them at the ladies tea tomorrow afternoon," she announced, the pride nearly bouncing off her as she spoke. "Two o'clock sharp. I'll save you a seat in the front row."

Then, before I could say a word, she turned off the light and marched back down the hallway toward the door.

Like it or not, it seemed I had a date for two o'clock on Saturday. Though she seemed a very far cry from the Proverbs 31 woman, I sensed God had arranged for me to "run into" Imogene and her dolls that day, and so I would follow through and see where it led.

I did attend and survive (just barely) the next afternoon's lecture about Imogene's dolls, despite the fact she insisted on giving us the story behind each one before we could make our escape. And I even learned from one of the other ladies in attendance (there were five of us, making for a doll-to-human ratio of about a million to one) that Imogene's husband had died 50 years earlier, only months after they had been married. She never remarried, never had children, and spent the remainder of her life collecting dolls. Though I didn't suddenly place Imogene on my potential role model list, I did understand her better after that day. I even asked her if she'd like to come in for an hour or so each week and help me (though I used the word "advise") with the bulletins. She did, and it became a regular ritual. In the process, I found myself wondering if sometimes the people who most resembled loose cannons in my life really just needed to be needed…and appreciated.

 Making It Personal

Have you ever "run into" someone who immediately made you want to run the other way, only to find out later that it was indeed a divine appointment? How did you handle the situation? If you stuck around to pursue the relationship, what did you learn? If you didn't, how do you think things might have turned out if you had?

"Therefore be merciful, just as your Father also is merciful. Judge not, and you shall not be judged. Condemn not, and you shall not be condemned."
—Luke 6:36–37

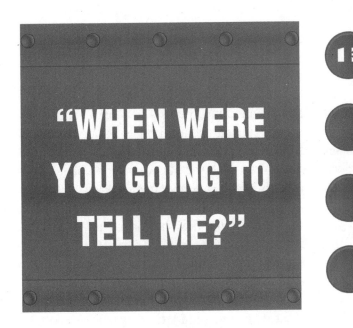

13

"WHEN WERE YOU GOING TO TELL ME?"

I think we should do a monthly newsletter," the pastor of the little church announced to me one day. "Not much—just a calendar of events and an announcement page. What do you think?"

OK, this was my boss as well as a pastor. Did I dare tell him what I really thought—that a church with nothing going on except a Sunday morning service, an occasional lecture on dolls, and a potluck now and then really doesn't need a newsletter? How would I ever find enough information to fill even a page or two?

I cleared my throat. "Well, I..."

"If you think it would be too much work to get it done in your current 12 hours, we'd be happy to extend your time and pay accordingly." He smiled and waited.

"Oh, it's not that." *I could probably do it in 5 minutes,* I thought, *but I doubt that's what he wants to hear.*

"Why don't you give it a try?" he suggested. "You type it and run the copies, and I'll call some of the ladies from the women's group to come in and help you fold and staple and get them into the mail."

I could see it now—an assembly line of blue-haired ladies, leaning on their walkers while they folded and stapled. I could hardly wait.

As it turned out, on the very first month there were actually five announcements—just enough that I couldn't get them plus the calendar all on one page. But if I started a second page to accommodate the leftover announcements, what would I do with the blank space on page two? I didn't dare omit any of the announcements, as each church member who came into the office to drop them off had let me know in no uncertain terms how important it was that the entire congregation was aware of their particular tidbit of breaking news. In all fairness, maybe it was important for everyone to know that the ice cream social had been moved from two o'clock to two-thirty on the second Saturday of the month.

As I sat at my desk, pondering my earth-shaking dilemma, it occurred to me that I should probably ask God what to do, and I had no sooner prayed than the answer popped right into my head. Of course! How long had I been wishing I could share my testimony about how God had saved me at the age of 26 and completely changed my life? This was the perfect opportunity.

I cleared it with the pastor first, who not only gave me the green light to write up and print my testimony in the newsletter but also told me to feel free to include other pieces in the future, so long as I ran them past him first. Wow! I'd been promoted from part-time church secretary and gopher to magazine—OK, newsletter—writer and editor. This could turn out to be a lot of fun!

I was right. I thoroughly enjoyed getting my testimony down on paper and run off on page two of the newsletter, just under the announcement for tryouts for the senior softball league. (I never even asked how that turned out.) Then I reminded the pastor of his offer to call in the troops to help me fold and staple. Unfortunately, we weren't able to recruit any of the members at the last minute, but we did manage to get the pastor's teenage granddaughter and a couple of her friends to help out, and the 100-plus copies of the not-quite-dead-yet congregational newsletter went out with the afternoon's mail.

Two days later I got my first review—compliments of congregational member Franklin T. (I have no idea what the T stood for, but apparently it had been considered part of his first name for so long that no one ever considered dropping it.)

"Did you write this?" he demanded, storming through the office door (as much as a 90-plus-year-old man on a cane can storm anywhere). He plopped a copy of the newsletter, opened to my story, on my desk.

I raised my eyebrows in surprise. I'd never been accosted by a nonagenarian before, and I wasn't sure how to react. I decided to go with honesty.

"Yes, I did. Why?"

Now it was Franklin T's turn to raise his eyebrows. "Why?" His leathery, road-mapped face was getting redder by the moment. "*Why*? I'll tell you why. I—" He stopped, studied me for a moment, and said, "No. On second thought, I won't tell you why. I'll tell Pastor instead. Tell him I'm here and I want to see him."

I didn't like the sound of that at all, but there was no way I could keep him from talking to the pastor if he'd already made up his mind—and apparently he had.

Standing on Holy Ground

I picked up the phone and buzzed my boss's office. "Franklin T is here, and...he wants to see you."

His sigh was long and loud. I imagined he'd had a run-in or two with Franklin T over the years. "What about?" he asked.

"I'm not sure...exactly...but I think it has something to do with what I wrote in the newsletter."

He was silent for a moment, and then asked, "You didn't put anything in besides what you already showed me, right?"

I assured him I hadn't, and then he told me to go ahead and bring Franklin T on back. I got up to lead the way, but he was already halfway there. I hurried along behind him, once again amazed at how quickly seniors could move when they wanted to. As he reached the office, the pastor opened the door and smiled in greeting.

"Franklin T! It's good to see you. Come on in."

He started to close the door behind Franklin T, but the agitated church member stopped him and looked back at me. "I want her here too."

Great. I was about to get my first literary review from someone nearly a hundred years old who walked with a cane and was loaded for bear. I was relatively certain it couldn't turn out well.

Once inside the pastor's office, I eyeballed the only chair in the room besides his and decided to stand and leave the spare for Franklin T, though from the look of things he wasn't about to sit down either. Still clutching the newsletter in his right hand, he presented it to the pastor in much the same way he had to me—by slamming it down on the desk.

"Did you know about this?" he demanded.

The pastor raised his eyebrows, looked from Franklin T to me and then back again, cleared his throat, and said, "Yes, I did."

Before he could say another word, Franklin T squinted his eyes and asked, "Is it true?"

The pastor frowned. "Is what true?"

"This," he sputtered, looking at him as if he were demented for not understanding the question. "All this she wrote about being 'saved' and 'born again' and 'repenting,' and how just going to church and trying to be a good person isn't enough. Is it true...or not?"

I found myself holding my breath, waiting almost as anxiously as Franklin T for the answer.

The pastor's face paled, and his mustache twitched. Finally he spoke. "Yes," he said, his voice uncharacteristically soft. He opened his mouth as if to say more, then closed it again.

I swallowed, my eyes darting back and forth between what suddenly seemed like hunter and prey. Then Franklin T spoke, his voice controlled but barely above a whisper.

"When were you going to tell me?" He paused before continuing, his voice rising slightly. "I'm 93 years old, Pastor. I've been sitting in this church listening to you preach every Sunday since you've been here." He leaned forward, resting his hands on the desk, his voice nearly booming now. "Just exactly when were you going to get around to telling me that I needed to repent and be born again if I wanted to get into heaven when I die?"

I knew my mouth was hanging open, but I just couldn't seem to will it shut again. Who would have thought my little story about how I got saved would stir up such a tornado of confrontation in this sleepy little church—and between Franklin T and the pastor, of all people? I wasn't too sure I'd have a job once the dust settled, but I didn't care. At that moment, eternity was on the line.

The next thing I knew, the three of us were standing in a circle, as tears coursed down Franklin T's face (and the pastor's and mine as well), and my formerly social-gospel-only boss led our elderly guest in the sinner's prayer. God used that incident to bring not only Franklin T but the pastor to a place of repentance. Franklin T, the oldest member of a seriously senior congregation, was born again, and the pastor confessed his fault in not preaching the gospel but rather having avoided any talk of repentance or sin or the need to be born again because he hadn't wanted to "offend anyone" in his flock.

I continued to work at the church as part-time secretary and overall gopher for several months, inserting an occasional story or article into the monthly newsletter and enjoying a comment or two from parishioners now and then, though I never had the sort of reaction I'd gotten from Franklin T.

And, though I'd like to say the church burst into full-blown revival and turned the city (or at least the neighborhood) on its ear as a result of my original newsletter article, I can't. But I can say this: Pastor, Franklin T, and I were never the same after that day. I'd learned the importance of not being "ashamed of the gospel of Christ, for it is the power of God to salvation for everyone who believes" (Romans 1:16).

 ## Making It Personal

Have you ever had an opportunity dropped in your lap to present the gospel? How did you react? What did you say? What were the results? Did you experience resistance or confrontation? Did your pride get in the way? How were you (or someone else) changed by the incident?

For I am not ashamed of the gospel of Christ, for it is the power of God to salvation for everyone who believes.
—Romans 1:16

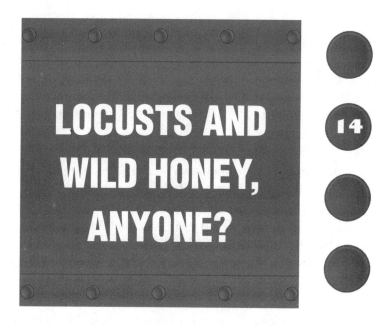

LOCUSTS AND WILD HONEY, ANYONE?

M y experiences with Mara and Imogene and Franklin T were continuing to impress upon my brain the message that it wasn't about me, but my heart was having a hard time making the transition. Now that God had used me to help bring a 93-year-old man to salvation, it was even harder to get my mind off of the "unholy trinity" of "me, myself, and I." It seemed the more I determined not to make "it" (meaning the world, the universe, and everything it contained) about me, the more I focused on self.

"Ugh!" I complained one day, as I sat at my kitchen table, sipping diet sodas with Linda, the so-called friend who had convinced me to join a gym. "Does it ever end? Do we ever really get over ourselves?"

She laughed. "Not on this planet. But we can never quit trying. Like John the Baptist said, 'He must increase, but I must decrease.' Why do you think he used the word 'must'? He knew it wouldn't be easy, and we'd fight it all the way."

I groaned. "Is that why he went around wearing camel-hair suits and eating bugs? I'd really rather not have to resort to that."

Linda laughed again. "Even if you did, it would just make it worse. You'd spend the rest of your life thinking about how miserable you were, so you'd still be focused on yourself."

"Thanks. I may not be any closer to getting over myself, but at least I can jettison the locusts-and-wild-honey option."

The problem wasn't that I didn't realize there was a problem. The problem was—well, the problem was *me*. I knew that, but what was I supposed to do about it? I really hadn't considered eating bugs or wearing camel hides as a solution, but where did that leave me? Was there no solution? How did other people do it? How did the Proverbs 31 woman become so spiritual, so perfect and mature that her own family—the ones who knew her better than anyone else— actually stood to their feet and called her blessed? In my family, among those who knew me best, I was usually just known as "she-who-drives-everyone-crazy" with whatever new "thing" I was into at the time. Talk about being a loose cannon.

I'm like a bulldog when I get my teeth into something. Even if it's something good, I don't always know when to let go. I chew on it, growl at anyone who tries to take it away, and—worst of all—insist everyone else should grab onto it as well.

I remember when I first heard of bran as the end-all and cure-all for humanity's ills. "It'll solve your stomach problems," I assured my aging parents. My dad glared at me and said he'd rather eat old shoes.

"It'll help us lose weight," I announced to my husband. He ignored me and ate another piece of pizza.

I resorted to exaggeration to win at least one convert. "It'll help you run faster and get better grades," I promised my youngest son Chris. But he scurried out the door, climbed a tree, and refused to come down until I promised never again to say the word *bran* in his presence. Though more than two decades have passed and Chris seldom hides in trees anymore, he retains a slight facial tick when anyone dares mention the "b" word—a tribute to my hysteria.

I, on the other hand, still eat bran, not because it has solved my stomach problems, helped me lose weight, or enabled me to run faster or get better grades, but because once I latched on to it as a positive thing I couldn't let go. It's become a matter of principle, though I can't imagine why.

Other "things" held my full attention for a time, but I did eventually give them up, at least to an extent. For instance, my exercise craze. I now understand that I didn't adopt exercise as a means to a healthier, more energetic lifestyle but simply because I was fast approaching my 40th birthday, and torturing myself with various exercise routines was a way of maintaining denial. Now, having survived my 60th birthday, I find I'm happy to take my daily lap around the senior park, where I still feel physically superior to those other seniors cruising around in their golf carts.

Getting Over Myself

Another "thing" I adopted during my "learning to run" years was Scripture memorization. Certainly a good thing, a wonderful, vital thing; the problem was that I managed to make it annoying by trying to force it on everyone else.

I was sure the more I memorized, the less I would focus on yours truly and the more like the Proverbs 31 woman I would become. I picked a new verse each week, typed it in large, bold letters, and taped it to every solid surface in our home and car. If you walked into the bathroom, there it was on the mirror. If you walked into the kitchen, there it was on the refrigerator and all the eye-level cupboards. If you walked into the living room, there it was on top of the TV, just above the screen. If you walked into the bedroom—any bedroom—there it was on the mirrors and closet doors.

That's where my family drew the line—and where I finally had to back down. I couldn't come up with a reason why my memory verse had to be in their bedrooms, though

I tried to convince them it was because I was obeying the biblical admonition in Numbers 6 to post God's commands on the doorposts and gates of our home.

"Fine," they agreed. "Post them on the doorposts and gates, and leave our bedrooms alone."

So I agreed to keep my Scripture-posting craze within my own boundaries; I was certain that later, when my family realized how much I'd matured as a result of having memorized so many Scriptures, they—like the Proverbs 31 family—would rise up and call me blessed. It was just a matter of time.

Wrong again. The more Scripture I memorized and spouted at every opportunity, the more everyone else ran for cover and resisted my attempts to get them to join me. They actually had the nerve to tell me I was becoming obnoxious about it!

"Isn't being a Christian supposed to make you a better person?" my self-proclaimed atheist dad growled when I tried to help him stop smoking by announcing that our bodies are to be treated as "temples of the Holy Spirit."

"Being a Christian means I'm forgiven," I explained, smugly paraphrasing a bumper sticker I'd recently seen. "It doesn't mean I'm perfect."

Dad snorted. "No kidding." He took a long drag on his cancer stick and said, "If being a Christian means you go around telling everybody else how to live, then leave me out. Seems to me that being a Christian should make you a little more considerate of others and a little less caught up in yourself." He shrugged. "But I don't claim to be one, so maybe I'm wrong."

Ouch. Not only had my unbelieving father just pointed out to me that I was more wrapped up in myself than ever, but he'd also let me know that my behavior was driving him away from God, rather than toward Him. That hurt. But then, the truth always does, doesn't it? It was enough to make even a bulldog like me sit up and take notice—and abandon my particular craze. Oh, I didn't stop memorizing Scripture, and I continued to post it where I could see it—on the front of my Bible, which I read every morning—but I no longer used it to beat everyone else over the head.

Once again, I'd come full circle—face-to-face—with the same problem: me. What was I to do about it? How did I stop thinking about and focusing on me?

I got some insight into that answer the next day. It was Sunday, and once again I was helping in one of the classrooms when I looked up and saw Mara. She walked in with her parents and made her way toward some empty seats near the back of the room. As my eyes riveted on her, her words of wisdom echoed in my memory: "I ask God every day why He loves me and why He's so good to me. I don't deserve it but He just loves me anyway."

He loves me anyway. In spite of myself... He loves me anyway. Though I spend 99 percent of my time focused on myself... He loves me anyway. Though He knows I'm weak... He loves me anyway.

So if God loves me anyway, why did I keep trying so hard? Was it really because I wanted to decrease so He could increase in me—or was I trying to prove something, trying to earn something? I wanted to believe my efforts were an honest attempt at focusing on God, but when I saw the simplicity of Mara's life and love for the Lord, I couldn't help but question my motives. If all my striving for spiritual maturity was really about trying to prove something, what was it I was trying to prove—and to whom was I trying to prove it?

Whatever my motives, it seemed the more I determined to learn and grow and become a mature disciple of Christ, a true Proverbs 31 woman who could control all those loose cannons on the ship called life, the more frustrated I became. I was running as fast as I could but getting nowhere. I was my own worst loose cannon. Would my Christian walk always be this way—trying and failing, trying harder and failing again?

It was obvious I wasn't going to find my answer eating bran, but surely God had a plan to teach me what I needed to learn... didn't He?

 Making It Personal

Think of times in your life when you seemed to be coming down from a spiritual high—something along the lines of being used by God to help bring someone to salvation. Can you think of something that happened soon after that caused you to doubt nearly everything you'd learned about God's working in your life? How did you react? Did you redouble your efforts to be "spiritual"? Were you tempted to throw your hands up in despair and resign from discipleship? How did you manage to regain your spiritual momentum?

● ● ● ● ●

"He must increase, but I must decrease."
—John 3:30

"DON'T FORGET TO WRITE"

15

That same Sunday morning, just at the moment of my greatest despair, an idea hit me: Mara modeled many of the qualities of the Proverbs 31 woman and though she may not be the mentor for me, Mara's own mentor was available. Of course, why hadn't I thought of her before? Mara's mother would be a perfect role model!

Was it possible she would have time to squeeze me in for an hour or two now and then, to allow me to sit at her feet and listen and learn? It was worth a try. I made the decision to catch up with her after class and ask. Surely she'd understand how important this was to me.

Mara's mother was a charming lady, born and raised in the South and oozing gentility and grace. Her name was Rose, which didn't surprise me. This woman was not only attractive, but she smelled good too. There was a natural sweetness and wisdom about her that convinced me I'd finally found my Proverbs 31 woman.

That she was so receptive to my bumbling request to talk with her had impressed me almost as much as her gracious persona. I'd approached Rose after class and mumbled something about how much I'd appreciated Mara's previous comments about Jesus's amazing and unconditional love for us. She smiled and nodded and started to walk away, but stopped when I cleared my throat and said I had a favor to ask.

"I...wonder if you might...be willing to talk to me some time."

She looked puzzled, as she glanced from me to her husband and Mara, who stood waiting for her outside the classroom. They were busy talking with someone, so apparently she felt it was all right to spend a couple of minutes with me.

"Certainly, my dear," she said, her warm smile putting me at ease. "What would it be concerning?"

"It's..." I felt the heat rising from my neck to my cheeks, that hated blush that had plagued me since I was a kid. "I've...been trying to find someone to talk to about...the Proverbs 31 woman." I returned her smile and tried to ignore my burning cheeks. "I thought you might...be able to help me with that."

Despite my pitiful explanation, she graciously accepted, inviting me to her home two days later. So there I was, sitting across from her at the kitchen table, my hands wrapped around a mug of cocoa in an effort to ward off the lingering chill that had seeped into my bones during the trip from my home to hers on this unseasonably cold spring day.

"I really appreciate your taking the time to talk with me," I said. "I know you must be busy, and I won't keep you long."

Rose smiled, the skin around her warm brown eyes crinkling slightly. "Take all the time you need. I'm never too busy to talk with someone about the Scriptures. I've always admired the Proverbs 31 woman." She chuckled and added, "Though I can't imagine keeping up with her schedule or living up to her example."

I raised my eyebrows. "You can't? But...I thought... you have Mara, and this beautiful home, and..."

Rose's eyes softened. "I do have so much, don't I? God has blessed me so richly."

"I didn't mean that," I said, rushing to explain myself. "Your home is beautiful—and so is Mara, of course. But...what I meant was, you do so much, and you do it so well. That's what made me think of you and the Proverbs 31 woman. You seem so much like her—"

Rose's melodic laugh interrupted me, as she reached across the table to place a hand on my arm. "Oh, my dear, I'm sorry. Forgive me, please. I'm not laughing at you, truly, but..." She shook her head as she regained her composure. "I suppose I was just caught off-guard by your comparison of me to a woman I've always considered somewhat of a role model myself, though an unachievable one, I'm afraid."

I was shocked. Rose thought of the Proverbs 31 woman as a role model, just as I did; more astonishing was the fact that she felt she could never live up to this scriptural superwoman anymore than I could. If someone like Rose couldn't achieve Proverbs 31 status, what hope was there for me?

"But," I paused, unsure how to continue but unable to accept my pursuit of spiritual superwoman status as a lost cause. "Shouldn't we at least try to emulate the Proverbs 31 woman? Surely her example is worth pursuing...isn't it?"

Rose's face softened. "Certainly it is. Any godly example in scripture is worth emulating. We're instructed in 1 Timothy 6:11 to pursue righteousness, godliness, faith, love, patience, and gentleness, but these attributes are fruits of the Spirit, characteristics of God Himself, so the only way to pursue them is to pursue a deeper relationship with Jesus—to seek more of Him and less of us."

There was that "it's not about me" message again. I knew that—at least, I thought I did—but if I knew it, why did I keep feeling like such a failure each time I heard it?

"How do we do that? I know it's not about me; it's about Him. I know we must decrease and He must increase, but...how do we do it?"

Rose smiled. "In our own strength we can't. That's the frustrating part. If left to ourselves, it will always be about us, even when we try to do something good. The only things we can change are outward things—words, behavior, circumstances." She stopped and tapped her hand against her chest, right over her heart. "We can't change what's really important. Only God can do that. That's why His Spirit comes to live inside us when we receive Him as Savior, so He can change us from the inside out."

Less Doing, More Becoming

Everything Rose said made sense, and I readily accepted and believed it. But what about becoming like the Proverbs 31 woman? Doesn't emulating someone mean we should try to act like that person?

When I posed that very question, she said, "Of course it does. Where do you think the what-would-Jesus-do craze came from? It's the idea that we should act and behave like Jesus. But the problem is that when we try just by human strength and will to walk as He walked and talk as He talked and live as He lived, we fail miserably. It isn't about doing what He did; it's about being who He is."

Now I was really confused. Jesus was a man, but He was also God. How can we "be" who He is?

My cocoa was cooling fast, so I took a sip to buy a little time. As I waited, Mara walked into the room.

"Hello," she said shyly, sidling close to her mother as she peered down at me. "I'm Mara."

"I know. I've seen you in Sunday school."

Recognition lit her dark eyes, and she grinned. "You're Kathi, the lady that writes on the board and staples papers together and stuff like that."

She had me pegged. "That's me. And you're the lady who reminded us all how much Jesus loves us."

She flushed a rosy pink and nodded. "That was the first song my mom taught me when I was little, 'Jesus Loves Me.'

I'm glad she did 'cause now, no matter what happens or what anybody says or does, I know it doesn't matter 'cause Jesus still loves me."

Hot tears pricked the back of my eyelids. I could only imagine some of the things that had been said to Mara through the years, but what an anchor she had to hold onto, thanks to a very wise mother. Rose might not believe she could reach Proverbs 31 status, but it looked like she'd come as close as anyone could.

"Your mom is a very special lady," I said, fighting the tears that threatened to squeeze out and drip down my face.

Mara nodded, and her face lit up. "Yep. And I'm going to be just like her some day."

I gave up. A couple of tears escaped, and there was nothing I could do about it.

Mara looked alarmed. "Are you OK?" she asked, moving toward me and placing her hands on my shoulders.

"I'm fine. Really. I just..."

Mara looked at her mother. "Mom, let's pray for Kathi."

Rose reached across the table and laid her hand on mine, while Mara's hands stayed on my shoulders and she began to speak.

"God, help my friend," she prayed. "I think she's sad about something, and I don't know what it is, but You do. Could You give her a kiss, Jesus, like You do for me sometimes, and let her know You're taking care of everything?"

What felt like a feather brushed my cheek, and a sense of electricity shot down my spine as Mara gave a resounding "amen." The simplicity of her prayer burned in my heart as surely as the Father's lip-prints burned on my cheek.

"Thank you, Mara," I whispered. "How did you know exactly what I needed?"

Mara shrugged. "I didn't. But God did, and He always tells me in my heart what to do and say."

I glanced at Rose, whose eyes glistened. She turned her eyes in my direction and said, "The Proverbs 31 woman needed encouragement too. She needed people to love her and pray for her, just like we do."

I nodded. Maybe she was right. Maybe the Proverbs 31 woman was more like us than I'd realized. Maybe she too struggled with insecurities and uncertainties and feelings of failure. Maybe she had a role model whose example seemed unattainable. Yet God commended her and listed her many accomplishments in the Bible, so she must have done something right.

As Rose walked me to the front door an hour later, Mara called to me from the stairway, "Goodbye, Kathi! Come back some time...and don't forget to write!"

I stopped, puzzled, and gazed up at the dark-haired young woman with the guileless smile. What had she meant by that? Did she want me to write her a note, or...?

Again she shrugged, turning to walk back up the stairs, and said, "I don't know what it means. I just know God told me in my heart to say it."

I stored those words in my own heart, pondering them all the way home.

 Making It Personal

Have you ever had someone pray for you in just the right way, as only God's Spirit could have directed him or her? How did that situation turn out? Looking back on that time now, is it possible it may have been a turning point in your life?

He makes intercession for the saints according to the will of God.
—Romans 8:27

Learning to Fly—Soaring with Eagles

[B]ut those who hope in the LORD will renew their strength. They will soar on wings like eagles.
—Isaiah 40:31 (NIV)

Up, Up, and Away!

Ever since I first read the 40th chapter of Isaiah, I had dreamed of the day when I'd finally be a mature enough Christian to soar with eagles. It seemed I'd wasted the better part of my life hanging out with a bunch of turkeys, and I longed for a promotion. When the opportunities finally came, I couldn't have been more amazed.

For as long as I can remember I've had a love affair with words, and to say I've always been an avid reader is a serious understatement. More than once my mother caught me, long after bedtime, hiding under my blankets with a flashlight, lost in the adventures of the "boxcar kids" or Nancy Drew. It was a natural transition to progress from reading stories to writing them. By the time I was in my teens I was working on the school newspaper, getting As in English and creative writing, and winning awards in the school's annual writing contest.

My passion for words increased over the years, so when I became a Christian in my 20s I immediately decided I would devote my life to writing books for God. A lofty goal, but one that I forgot to consult God about before banging on publishers' doors. As a result, they all slammed shut in my face. Discouraged, I whined at God, only to hear Him whisper to my heart, "You'll be ready to write for Me when you're ready to write books without your name on them."

I had no idea what that meant, and being a spiritual rug rat at the time, I was quickly distracted with other pursuits and activities. I left my "I want to write for God" dream on the back burner, as I progressed from rug rat to toddler to runner. Other than writing an occasional newsletter article for the church where I worked, my passion for words was on hold. Then, not long after Mara admonished me with the words "don't forget to write," I landed a word-related job as an editorial assistant in the curriculum department of a Christian publishing house. It didn't pay much and had few fringe benefits, but it was about as close to heaven as I imagined any job on earth could be. I could almost feel the wind beneath my wings.

One day, as I sat in my minicubicle, checking punctuation and verifying Bible verses, the publisher came in and sat down beside me. When he greeted me by name, I was flabbergasted. I'd seen him wandering the halls a few times, but we'd never spoken to one another, and I certainly had no reason to think he knew my name. I realized I should say something intelligent and respectful, but "uh…hello" was the best I could do.

"I understand you have a way with words," he said, no doubt hoping I did better as a scribe than a speaker. I thought of trying to redeem myself by saying something brilliant, but then I remembered Abraham Lincoln's admonition that "it's better to remain silent and be thought a fool than to open your mouth and remove all doubt." I pressed my lips together and managed a nod.

A flicker of doubt danced through his eyes, and I imagined he was making a mental note to fire the person who recommended me. Valiantly, he pressed on. "I wondered if you might like to try your hand at a freelance writing project."

I sat up a bit taller and raised my eyebrows to indicate interest.

"We need a writer to work with one of our authors on a special project. Though he'll be supplying all the information, you'll actually be writing the book; it just won't have your name on it."

When I finally opened my mouth and shouted, "I'd love to! When do I start?" the poor man nearly catapulted out of his chair.

"My assistant will be in touch," he promised, and then hurried down the hallway in the direction of his office, never to return to my cubicle.

True to his word, he had his assistant contact me with the details, and before I knew it I was soaring, as I took the first step in the fulfillment of my dream, just as God had whispered to my heart so many years earlier: I would write books for Him when I was ready to do so without my name on them. I had been too immature to understand what He meant then, but now it was clear. After coming through a season of spiritual running, when I'd learned that nothing was about me and everything was about Him, I was finally ready to fly.

A CHANGE IN FLIGHT PLANS

16

Once I took off, there was no stopping me. Very soon after that first freelance job for my publisher, the brave man gave me more writing opportunities, one of them being my first "real" book. It was a women's devotional, a compilation of personal stories from women of all ages, geographical regions, and spiritual stages of life. I would cocompile this book with another editor, my dear friend and fellow lover-of-words, Mary.

We were thrilled, taking every possible opportunity to turn lunchtime into planning sessions at our favorite restaurant, known for its delicious pies. We had so many planning sessions and ate so much pie that we soon began to refer to ourselves as the "Fat and Famous Duo." (It was funny then because we were still young and slim; the passing of time and the pull of gravity have tweaked our sense of humor, and we now agree we are dangerously close to fulfilling the first half of our title and never accomplishing the second.) But we were about to become authors (my first book with my name on it!), and the publisher had fronted us a whopping $500 advance—each! That's a lot of pie.

Within a few short months we'd amassed a great collection of devotional stories from women all over the country— some with household names, others whose names were known only within their own households. One of the more prominent names was Shirley Dobson, whose husband, Dr. James Dobson, preordered enough copies of our devotional book that we zoomed right up to the top of our publisher's best seller list. On top of that, Dr. Dobson advertised it in his magazine and announced it on his program every day for an entire month. You can't buy better advertising than that!

We were on our way, soaring about as high as any two on-the-way-to-being-fat-and-famous eagles dared to venture. While riding that updraft, I decided to throw out some other book ideas, not only to my current publisher/employer but to other publishers as well. Very quickly I developed a reputation for being able to submit my laundry list and get a book contract. I was cranking them out as fast as I could write them and the publishers could get them into print.

There was only one problem. The books weren't selling very well. I was devastated. I'd been so sure I had this marketing thing figured out. You wrote a book, sent it to Focus on the Family, and then worked on the next book while you waited for the royalties and accolades to roll in. Instead, I soon got the dreaded "negative royalty" statement in the mail.

How could that be? Surely there was some sort of mistake. Maybe someone hit the wrong key and typed a minus sign instead of a plus. A call to the publisher assured me there'd been no mistake. More copies of my first "great American novel" had been returned than sold. I was crushed. The wind beneath my wings had become dead air, and I was sinking fast.

Then Linda, the friend who talked me into joining the gym and listened to me whine about not being able to "get over myself," came up with another idea. To that point, despite the gym membership fiasco, I'd basically considered Linda a relatively intelligent and levelheaded person, but my opinion quickly changed as she told me what I should do to bolster my book sales.

"People need to know you're out there," she explained.

I know now I should have stopped her then and asked exactly where "out there" was, since I've always wondered and it would have been a great way to change the subject before she really went off the deep end. Unfortunately, I didn't say anything and lost my window of opportunity. To this day I've never discovered where "out there" is, and the next thing I knew she was talking about the well-known but otherwise unidentifiable "they," who obviously inhabit some uncharted location "out there." That's about the time I realized the conversation was heading in a direction I did not want to go.

"They need to know you have some great books that would really bless and encourage them," Linda continued. "I was thinking that if you started going around to different church and civic groups and speaking about your books, then…"

Her mouth was still moving, but I no longer heard her. My brain shut down at the word "speaking." How could I have been so wrong about someone? Where had I gotten the idea that this so-called friend actually knew me? Very obviously she didn't, or she wouldn't have used the "s" word in reference to something she thought I should do. My head was reeling, and I could hear my heart pounding in my ears, but I knew I had to pull myself together and tell her exactly why her idea was the worst one to come down the pike since the unveiling of the Yugo.

Linda was still talking, her enthusiasm growing as she expounded on her plan to launch me into public speaking. I held up my hand. "Stop," I said, feeling very much like a helpless traffic cop trying to halt a runaway 18-wheeler. "I don't do that."

She frowned. "Don't do what?"

"Speaking. I don't speak to people."

Her frown deepened. "That's ridiculous. You're speaking to me. What am I, a telephone pole?"

"Very funny. You know what I mean. I don't speak to large groups of people, meaning two or more."

"Even more ridiculous. I thought your goal in taking all those classes and helping out with Sunday School was so you could teach a class yourself. How are you going to do that if you don't speak to more than two people at a time?"

Facing Down My Fears

She had me on that one. In fact, it was something I'd been worrying about a lot lately, especially now that I had completed enough of my ministry classes that the pastor had told me I could sign up to teach a class in the fall. Somehow it had seemed so much easier in the beginning, before I sat down and analyzed the requirements of teaching, one of which was standing in front of a classroom full of people and speaking to them. I'd actually been reconsidering my ministry direction lately, thinking I might prefer getting involved in some other area—something behind the scenes, something where I didn't have to risk making a fool of myself....

That was the real problem, but there were some things I wasn't ready to admit to anyone, including my well-meaning friend with the overactive imagination and harebrained ideas.

"I'll deal with that situation when I come to it," I said. "Besides, that's really not the issue here. You're talking about me going out on some half-baked lecture tour, selling my books like I was hawking snake oil—"

"Oh, please," she said, interrupting my tirade. "Don't you think you're overreacting a bit? I didn't say anything about a lecture tour. No offense, but you're not that big a deal. Lecture tours are for people with credentials and well-known names. Sorry, but that's just not you."

We all know when we've been nailed with the truth, and besides, I asked for that one. But that didn't make it hurt any less. I may not have wanted to do public speaking, but I didn't want anyone telling me I'd have a tough time getting invited to do so at anything bigger than a Tupperware party.

"Fine," I conceded. "So what's this big idea of yours? If no one would come and hear me speak, why should I even try? How is it going to help my book sales if I go somewhere to speak and no one shows up? It would be embarrassing."

She laid her hand on my arm. "Weren't you just telling me the other day how you've been learning that it's not about you, it's about God? All I'm saying is, why not at least pray about this and see what happens." She shrugged. "Hey, your books aren't selling anyway, so what have you got to lose?"

I forced a smile, hoping to placate her and put an end to this pointless and humiliating conversation. "All right, I'll pray about it. If God tells me I'm supposed to do public speaking, I will." I figured it was a safe assumption that God wasn't about to send the angel Gabriel to announce to me that I needed to start public speaking, so that was the end of that.

Two weeks later my pastor approached me, grinning from ear to ear. "Remember when you told me you wanted to teach one of the adult Sunday school classes? I've just come from a meeting with the elders, and we voted unanimously to start a new class for those who'd like to write articles and stories for our church newsletter. We want you be the teacher, especially since I know you have experience doing newsletters, not to mention the books you've published these last few years. I think we could fill a classroom to overflowing with a subject like that. What do you think?"

I've never actually seen a deer caught in the headlights before, but I think at that moment I did a great imitation of one. My pastor probably assumed I was so overcome with joy that I didn't know what to say. After a moment of silence, I managed to squeak out one word: "When?"

"As soon as possible. How about two weeks from Sunday? It won't take much preparation on your part. You've got the education and the experience, and if I announce it from the pulpit and we get it into the bulletin right away, I think we'll have a great response." He shook his head in obvious amazement. "Isn't it something the way God puts things together? Here you couldn't wait to teach a class, and now that you're ready, we have a new class that's just tailor-made for you. The message couldn't be clearer if God sent the angel Gabriel himself to tell you about it." He chuckled as he turned to walk away.

I watched him disappear around the corner, as his words about the angel Gabriel rang in my ears. I'd been ambushed, and there was nothing I could do about it—unless I wanted to disobey a direct order from God. I'll admit it crossed my mind, but as terrified as I was about accepting this divine assignment, I was more terrified of refusing it. I was stuck, thrust into the arena of public speaking, whether I liked it or not. No doubt Linda would be happy when I told her about it, though I doubted a Sunday School class was the proper venue to try to increase my book sales.

I couldn't understand it. Why would God choose someone like me, who nearly fainted every time I had to stand up in grammar school and give a book report? Didn't God remember the "deal" I'd made with Him when I accepted Jesus as my Savior? I hadn't thought about it in years, but I'd had no reason to until now—now when I was being thrown to the wolves.

"Remember, God?" I prayed. "Remember how I said I'd do anything for You—except public speaking?"

The only sound I heard in response was the faint rustling of wind, inviting me to spread my wings once again....

 **Making It Personal**

What seemingly insurmountable challenges do you face in your life today? How are you handling them? How can God's ability in the face of your inability make a difference?

● ● ● ● ●

I can do all things through Christ who strengthens me.
—Philippians 4:13

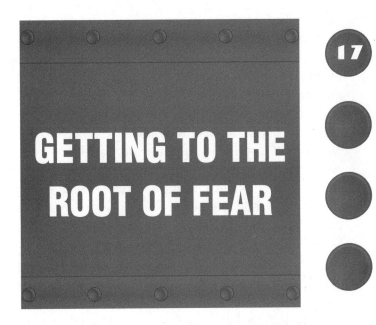

GETTING TO THE ROOT OF FEAR

In just over a year I'd quickly adapted to writing and publishing and thought my life was finally sailing along on smooth seas, straight into the Proverbs 31-woman tight-ship port, and then I was capsized by what I called the "public-speaking demon." To say I was nervous as I stood before those 23 people who showed up for my first class would be the understatement of the century. Though I knew several of them from various ministries and church functions, I felt as if I were standing on the edge of the Grand Canyon, waiting to dive off headfirst, while these eager spectators cheered me on.

I managed the meet-and-greet portion of the session, welcoming people at the door and inviting them to find a seat, all the while smiling as if there were nowhere else on earth I'd rather be. Then it was time to begin; I could no longer postpone the inevitable.

This is ridiculous, I told myself, as I woodenly placed one foot in front of the other and made my way to the front of the classroom, my smile still attached to my frozen face. *You know the topic. You wrote for and edited the church newsletter at work long enough that you should be able to handle any questions they throw at you about that, and you've taken plenty of creative writing classes over the years, not to mention publishing several books, and now finishing the ministry classes.*

However, in all honesty, I knew it wasn't my qualifications—or lack thereof—that was causing the mass attack of butterflies in my stomach or the buzzing in my ears. It was just plain fear of opening my mouth and having nothing come out, of standing there, dumbstruck, in front of all those people and wishing the floor would open up and swallow me right there on the spot. I was about to open my mouth and announce to the world that I was indeed a fool who should have known better and stayed home.

This is ridiculous. What is it they say? Ninety-nine percent of our fears never materialize. Of course, there's always the chance this could be that one percent....

I stepped behind the podium and arranged my papers—all 73 sheets. How much time did I think I had anyway? Unless I planned to talk really fast, there was no way I was going to make a dent in the pile of notes I'd brought with me. But somehow working on those notes all week had helped keep my fears under control. Now those fears were descending on me with a vengeance. My knees were buckling, my stomach was churning, and my mouth felt like the Sahara Desert. Why hadn't I thought to bring a glass of water with me?

I swallowed, opened my mouth, and managed to croak, "Welcome." I cleared my throat and tried again. "I'm so glad you all came."

I sounded like a centuries-old mummy with sand in my mouth, but at least I was talking. Still wishing I had some water, I decided to press on. What did I have to lose? I was already up there, and everyone seemed to be tuned in and listening.

Halfway through my undoubtedly boring pronouncement of my dubious qualifications to teach the class, I was astonished to see Mara and her mother sneak into the back of the classroom and quietly take a seat. Over the last few years since I'd begun writing and publishing books, my friendship with Mara and Rose had deepened; now their smiles warmed my heart, and I began to speak with a bit more confidence. Then I noticed Mara get up and slip out of the room. I stumbled and stammered before regaining my composure—such as it was—and wondered what I'd said that had spurred her to leave.

When she returned, I had my answer. Mara had brought me a glass of water. Smiling sweetly, she handed it to me, and I gratefully accepted her offering and promptly chugged more than half of it before she had time to return to her seat. I figured the secret was out and my dignity gone by then anyway, so why not make the best of it and at least be able to speak without a swollen tongue?

Things seemed to improve after that, and by the end of the session most of the class had joined in a lively question-and-answer period. When the bell rang, signaling the end of the hour, I hadn't even made it to page two of my notes! Had I said anything intelligent the entire time? Would anyone feel it was worthwhile to return the following week?

Is God Good or Not?

As it turned out, the class nearly doubled in size by week two, and I soon found myself eagerly anticipating each get-together with my "students," though I had to admit I was learning as much from them as they were from me. The only ones who dropped out were Mara and Rose, who never returned after the first week.

"We just came to support you," Rose explained when I dropped by their house to inquire about their absence after week two. "It was Mara's idea. She thought you might be scared."

I started to protest that I hadn't been scared at all, but when I looked from Rose to Mara, whose smile radiated her delight at being able to help, I knew the jig was up.

"You're right. I was scared. I think I still am, but not as much. It helped so much to see you both sitting out there, and I so appreciated that glass of water you brought, Mara."

Mara nodded. "I know. I get scared sometimes—and thirsty too. I thought of how I'd feel if I was standing up there, and that's when I knew I should get you some water." She smiled again. "You did real good after you had your drink, and I could understand you better too."

I laughed out loud, and so did Rose. Before long Mara joined us, and we didn't stop until Rose pulled herself together enough to offer us some lemonade. As the three of us sat at the kitchen table sipping her homemade brew, we discussed our fears and why we sometimes let them beat us.

"It's because we're so busy thinking about ourselves," I suggested. "At least, I think that's the problem in my case. I'm so worried about what people are going to think, or what will happen if I fail."

"With me," Rose said, "I have a tendency to imagine the tragic results of a worst-case scenario, even though there's no real reason to expect that to happen."

I could certainly relate to that. Then I noticed Mara, frowning slightly. Were we leaving her behind in our discussion?

Before I could think of a way to bring her back into the loop, she opened her mouth and said, "I think we're all afraid of the same thing."

Rose and I raised our eyebrows and waited.

"We think God isn't really good," Mara said.

You would have thought Rose's jaw and mine were connected, as they dropped in tandem. Because Rose knew Mara so much better than I, she had the good sense to wait and see what else her daughter would say. I, on the other hand, rushed right in like the proverbial fool I so often am.

"Oh, no, Mara. We know God is good. That's one of the main...things about God's personality." I had almost said "attributes" instead of "things," but I didn't want to talk over Mara's head.

She nodded and tapped her head. "We know it here," she said, and then moved her hand and tapped her chest. "But we don't know it here. If we did, we wouldn't be scared."

I swallowed, feeling like I'd been shot through the heart with a truth bullet. Who was talking over whose head now?

As Rose smiled and reached over to lay her hand on Mara's arm, tears flooded my eyes. *Here I go again. This is getting to be a bad habit.*

Before the tears could spill over onto my cheeks, Rose handed me a tissue. What was it about this family that had me either laughing or crying every time I turned around? It was their honesty, I decided. I couldn't think of a time when I'd been around people who were so openly honest about themselves. By the time I left that day, I knew I'd return to teach week number three of my class from an entirely different perspective.

As it turned out, I tossed my lesson plan for that week and had everyone pull their chairs into a circle, myself included. Then I asked them to talk about their fears of writing, the things that kept them from venturing out into the world of publishing. We heard the predictable answers, such as "fear of rejection." We also heard some surprising answers, such as "fear of success." That one made me laugh.

"I can relate to that," I said. "If I'd known that success in writing meant I'd have to start doing public speaking, I might never have put a pen to paper—or my fingers on a keyboard. I was absolutely petrified when we had our first class two weeks ago."

My vulnerability opened the door for some who had been holding back. Now the talk of fears began to get more personal, and before I knew it we were praying for one another, sharing tears and laughter, victories and defeat.

Then I shared what Mara had said a few days earlier. The class was as impressed by the truthfulness of her statement as I'd been. The remainder of the class period was spent looking up and reading Scriptures about fear, as well as about God's unconditional love and His perfectly trustworthy character.

When the bell rang I apologized for getting off track and not discussing the topic of writing, but the entire class responded with words of affirmation and the suggestion that we take it to the next level the following week. Armed with homework assignments, all of us—including myself—marched out the door, promising to return with an article about God's perfect love that casts out fear. It seemed an appropriate topic, as well as an appropriate way to apply it to our individual lives.

When I stopped by to tell Mara and Rose about it the next day, Mara was overjoyed. When I thanked her for getting it all started, she blushed. "It wasn't me. It was just what I heard God say in my heart."

And it was just what I needed to hear.

 Making It Personal

What are some of the fears that have plagued you in your lifetime? How do you think those fears held you back from the things God had for you? Have you dealt with those fears? If not, how do you suppose you could apply the truth of Mara's words to defeat those fears?

Whoever confesses that Jesus is the Son of God, God abides in him, and he in God.... God is love, and he who abides in love abides in God, and God in him.... There is no fear in love; but perfect love casts out fear.
—1 John 4:15–16,18

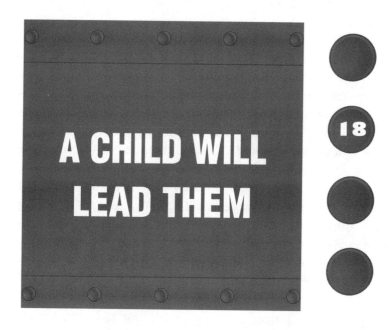

A CHILD WILL LEAD THEM

18

Some say we don't start feeling old until we realize our children are nearly grown and ready to begin their own lives. Suddenly we start sounding like our parents and uttering things like, "Where did the time go?"

Personally, I didn't start feeling old until I became a grandmother. Granted, that was relatively early, since my two older boys were both born before I was 20. But as the clan began to multiply, I understood the bumper sticker my dad sported on the back of his old blue Ford Escort for so many years: "If I'd known grandkids were so much fun, I'd have had them first."

He was right. Being a grandparent falls into an entirely different category than being a parent. It's all the fun without the responsibilities—which is exactly why we think our grandkids are the cutest, smartest, sweetest children on the face of the planet. When they're not, we give them back.

I'll never forget when I was visiting my daughter-in-law Christy and she invited me to accompany her and little Mikey to K-Mart. (If I remember correctly, my grandson's first words were "blue light special.") At that time Mikey was still in diapers, a true rug rat who zoomed around the house on his knees, stuck everything that wasn't tied down into his mouth, and drooled like he was getting paid by the gallon. I thought he was absolutely adorable, so when Christy suggested the outing, I snatched up my precious grandchild from the floor where he was diligently munching on the doggie kibble and carried him to the car. Christy grabbed her purse and raced out the door behind me. We were off!

We hadn't been strolling the aisles long before our pint-sized treasure started making those dreaded grunting noises that accompany a very red face. Not a great experience when you're in a public place, but one that goes with the territory of being a mom and a grandma, right?

By the time we pushed the baby-laden buggy to the back of the store where the overhead sign read "Restrooms," Mikey was no longer grunting or turning red, and the odor that wafted along behind us assured us he had done his business. When we got inside the restroom we realized we didn't have the diaper bag in the buggy. We quickly rehearsed what each of us brought from the house and soon realized the diaper bag wasn't in the car either. We had left it at home—and if ever we needed a clean diaper it was now.

"No problem," I said. "I'll run over to the baby section and grab a package. I'll be right back." (The alternative was that Christy would get the diapers, and I'd have to stay in the restroom and hold what was by now a very unhappy and odoriferous baby.)

I was back in minutes, though I'd forgotten to get a package of wipes. By that time neither of us was willing to hang on to Mikey while the other made another emergency run to the baby section, so Christy peeled off the offending diaper, tossed it into the trash, and washed Mikey off in the sink. Then we ran into our next problem: instead of paper towels, this environment-friendly facility had only blow-dryers. We turned one on and held his freshly washed behind up to the warm air.

Apparently this experience delighted him to no end (no pun intended) because he laughed and chortled through the entire event. He soon had us laughing as well. When a mother and her elementary-age daughter came into the bathroom and saw what we were doing, they looked horrified.

"Mom, what are they doing to the baby?" the little girl asked, her eyes wide and her face pale.

Her mother grabbed her by the arm and yanked her out the door, leaving Christy and me to wonder if store security would be called to arrest us. That didn't happen, but it was an experience we still laugh about today, nearly two decades later.

Lessons from Brittney

Then there was the time when I taught my granddaughter Brittney a new song. Brittney loved to sing, and she firmly believed that not only was I the most beautiful grandma in the world but I also had the best singing voice anywhere. (Wonder why I love this kid?) She was about three when I taught her to sing "Clementine," and sing it she did—at the top of her lungs. She'd open her mouth, throw her head back, and let loose with unending repetitions, until everyone ran screaming from the house.

The people on the plane weren't so lucky. Just a matter of days after I'd taught her the "Clementine" song, as she called it, Brittney and her mom got on a plane for what they and the other passengers thought would be a brief, uneventful two-hour flight. They'd no sooner lifted off from the runway than Brittney decided to entertain everyone with her new song. By the time they arrived at their destination, having heard slightly over 300 renditions of the same song as well as her perky explanation that her grandma had taught it to her, the passengers were forming a posse to track me down. Thankfully I was several hundred miles away.

One of the things I enjoyed most was taking my grandkids to church with me. Since Brittney lived closer than the rest of my grandchildren, she went with me most often. Her favorite time was Wednesday evening when she'd go to what she called "big kids' school" with the other three- and four-year-olds. Each week on the way into church we'd rehearse her memory verse, and each week on the way home she'd tell me about the story she heard in class.

One day when she was visiting me at my home, she became very frustrated with her toys and suddenly let loose with a string of words not fit to print. Two of those words were the precious name of Jesus Christ, used as curse words.

I was flabbergasted. Where had she heard such language?

When I asked her, she said she'd been visiting her mommy's friend, who was watching TV, and a man on the program screamed those words when he got mad. She undoubtedly assumed it was OK for her to do the same when she was upset.

I spent the next several minutes explaining to her that those are words we don't use, and that the people on TV shouldn't use them either. I then explained that the name of Jesus is very precious, and we should always be careful not to say it the wrong way, because it would hurt Jesus's feelings.

It was obvious from her wide-eyed attention that she was taking everything I said to heart, so I dropped the subject and never brought it up again...until one Wednesday night at church.

The service had ended and I went to retrieve Brittney from her classroom. The teacher met me at the door.

"I'm afraid I've upset Brittney," she said, "and I'm not sure why. I tried to get her to recite her memory verse, but she wouldn't."

I frowned, realizing she hadn't wanted to recite it for me either as we drove to church. That had never happened before.

"When I asked her why she didn't want to say it," the teacher continued, "she started to cry and said she didn't want to hurt Jesus' feelings. Does that make any sense?"

The light came on, and I asked, "Does the verse have the name of Jesus Christ in it?"

When the teacher nodded, I understood the problem—and gave Brittney a clearer explanation of when and how to speak the name of Jesus, and when not to. I also elaborated on why we shouldn't say any words that hurt anyone's feelings, and she seemed to understand. I was sure the problem was solved.

Then the tables were turned. Brittney and I were riding to church a couple of weeks later when suddenly a car full of teenagers came speeding up behind us on a two-lane road and crossed the double yellow lane to pass us, laughing as they flew by and nearly knocking us off the road.

"Idiot!" The word was out of my mouth before I realized it, and I quickly pulled off to the shoulder to give my heart time to return to its normal rate. My hands were still shaking when I heard Brittney say, "Grandma, you don't 'posed to say that."

I looked at her, surprised. What had I said?

Idiot.

The word echoed in my ears, and I felt the heat rise to my cheeks. Her big brown eyes were fixed on me, and I realized she had no clue that we'd nearly been in an accident. All she knew was that her grandma had just called someone an idiot. She may not have known what an idiot was, but she knew I hadn't meant it as a compliment.

Still, it wasn't as if I'd actually cursed—was it? Idiot may not be a kind word, but it wasn't really a curse word either, and it certainly described the person who'd barreled past us at twice the speed of light, laughing and nearly catapulting us into a ditch. Hadn't I shown restraint in not saying something worse?

I opened my mouth to defend myself, only to stop short as I gazed into those big brown eyes, trusting and waiting for me to do the right thing.

It was worse than when I'd stood in front of that room full of people at church, as they watched and waited for me to teach that first class. That was important, yes—but this was so much more so.

"Thank You, God," I prayed silently, "for speaking to me through this little child. Help me now to say and do the right thing."

I took a deep breath and cleared my throat, then managed to croak, "You're right, Brittney. I'm not supposed to say that, am I?"

Her nod was barely perceptible. She was still waiting.

"Should we pray and tell Jesus I'm sorry?" I asked.

Her smile broke through, and her nod was confident, as we joined hands and prayed.

"Forgive me, Jesus," I said. "I was scared, and I said a bad word. Help me not to say that ever again. And help that young man who was driving so fast to slow down. Protect him and all his passengers. Most of all, help them to come to know You."

"Amen!" Brittney yelled, and then clapped her hands in joy.

"Amen," I agreed, realizing I'd just learned an important lesson on public speaking from a very honest three-year-old.

 Making It Personal

Can you think of instances in your own life where the innocence and honesty of a child opened your eyes to a truth God was trying to show you? How did you react? Could you have handled those instances differently and possibly changed the outcome?

"Therefore whoever humbles himself as this little child is the greatest in the kingdom of heaven."
—Matthew 18:4

"WHO'S SHE?"

19

I'd been humbled again—by a three-year-old—and I was determined to maintain that humble position. But as book contracts and speaking invitations continued to come my way, I could feel the ego meter rising.

Nevertheless, God had ways to keep me humble in spite of myself—like my experience with Rosey Grier. Famous for being one of the two bodyguards who captured Sirhan Sirhan immediately after Senator Robert Kennedy was shot, Rosey had also been an All-Pro for the New York Giants and one of the Los Angeles Rams' "Fearsome Foursome" football greats—the only one, so far as I know, who also enjoyed doing needlepoint.

It all started when a publisher called me one day and said, "If you're free for lunch tomorrow, I'd like you to join me and Rosey Grier to discuss the possibility of the two of you doing a book together."

Now I'll admit that I didn't become an avid football fan until slightly after Rosey's playing days, but I certainly recognized his name. Even my mother, who wouldn't know a touchback from a touchdown, knew who he was. Intrigued,

I quickly agreed, then called my oldest son, Al, the most devoted football fan of all time.

"You'll never guess who I'm having lunch with tomorrow," I said.

"Who?" he asked, stifling a yawn. This wasn't the first time his goofy mother had called him to announce one of her harebrained schemes, and none of them so far had managed to excite him in the least. I was sure this time it would be different.

"Rosey Grier," I said, and then waited expectantly.

"Who's she?"

It was the first time the term "generation gap" had hit me between the eyes with the force of a meat cleaver. Who's *she*? I opened my mouth to explain, and then closed it again. The impact would obviously be lost in the translation.

I went to the meeting, and the next thing I knew, Rosey and I were signing a contract to do a book that would contain a compilation of testimonies and favorite sports memories from some of the top Christian athletes in the country. Rosey's job would be to contact those otherwise unreachable celebrities and set up the interviews; I would then do the interviews, either in person or over the phone, and write them up for the book.

Everything progressed smoothly. I began to do some phone interviews and was impressed at the depth of what many of these athletes had to say. One day, however, I walked in the front door, carrying a bag of groceries, when my youngest son, Chris, a teenager at the time and the only son living at home, called out, "Mom, somebody named Roger Starbuckle is on the phone for you."

I dropped the groceries, mortified, and snatched the receiver from my perplexed son. My embarrassment obviously showed in my voice, because as soon as I put the receiver to my ear and started to apologize, the laugh on the other end of the line grew louder and more robust.

"That's a good one," he finally managed between guffaws.

"Roger Starbuckle! I'll have to remember that."

Please don't, I thought to myself. Aloud I said, "I'm so sorry, Mr. Staubach. I—"

"Hey," he interrupted, "don't worry about it. I have kids too."

We did the interview, and the project continued.

One day soon after, I received a call from Rosey's wife, Margie, inviting me to join her and Rosey in Phoenix at a conference for Christian athletes. "Many of the Christian athletes you and Rosey need to interview will be here in this one place," she said. "It's perfect."

She was right, and I hopped on a plane and flew to Phoenix. When I caught a cab at the airport and told the driver where I wanted to go, he began to eye me curiously in the rearview mirror. Finally he asked, "What sport do you play?"

I stifled a laugh and the temptation to tell him I was a wrestler. "I'm a writer," I explained, "here to do interviews."

His interest dissipated quickly, but he got me safely to my destination. While there I was able to do enough interviews for more than half the book. One of them was especially memorable, as I sat and talked with Barry Sanders, the newly drafted Detroit Lions star. Scarcely 19 years old and with a megacontract in his lap, this young man astounded me with his wisdom and humility.

For starters, he brought his parents with him to the conference, and they joined us for the interview. "The first thing I'm going to do," Barry said, "is get a new house for my mom and dad. Then I'm going to continue doing what I've been doing all my life—finding out who I am apart from football. I could break a bone and lose my career in an instant. If I allow football to define me, then who would I be if I lost my ability to play? I want to find out who God created me to be, and then be the very best I can at whatever that is."

Another powerful reminder from someone much younger than I—a reminder I told myself I wouldn't forget.

Swallowing My Pride

Then the book was released, and we had our first book-signing event. I'd had book-signings before, since I'd already published several books of my own by then, but this was different. People actually came to this one—in droves! By the time I arrived at the venue, people were lined up around the block. Somehow I knew it wasn't because I was going to be there.

Rosey and I sat behind a table, pens in hand and a mound of books in front of us. When the doors opened and the stampede began, it was a bit scary. Rosey was first at the table, and he signed books as he greeted people, then passed the books to me so I too could sign, since both our names were on the front. The people, however, weren't interested in my signature. Once they had his, they snatched up their books and headed out the door.

I kept smiling and nodding at people, wishing I could run out the door with Rosey's escaping fans, until my gracious coauthor noticed what was happening.

"Here," he said, "let's change seats. That way they can get your signature first."

It worked, though people looked at me as if wondering, *Who are you and why are you signing my book?* But they allowed me to do so just so they could get to Rosey and obtain his autograph. (It seemed not everyone was as ignorant of Rosey's identity as my oldest son!)

In spite of the humbling reminder that few people knew or cared about my part in writing that book, it still seemed my life as a believer was off and running. I may not have become the perfect Proverbs 31 woman, but time and experience was teaching me much of what I needed to learn.

As it turned out, the book was nominated for an Angel Award from Excellence in Media, no small honor in the publishing world. The event was complete with black ties, stretch limos, and paparazzi galore. When the winners for our particular category were announced and our book was among them, we quickly made our way to the stage. I was pleased that I managed the walk without tripping or doing anything else klutzy—and then they announced our names: "Rosey Grier and Linda Holland."

Huh? I'd had a name change and no one told me? Then I realized what had happened. Linda Holland was the publisher's representative for *Winning*. She was the one who'd submitted our book for nomination and had somehow been listed as Rosey's coauthor.

I now had to make a choice: compound the problem (and my embarrassment) by making the correction over the microphone—or accepting my angel and returning to my seat as Linda Holland. I opted for the latter. After all, almost no one in the audience knew or cared if my name was Kathi or Linda, nor would they remember the incident after it was over. I, however, would remember it for a very long time.

The incident gave me an entirely new perspective on my son Al's comment about Rosey Grier: *Who's she?* I remembered then how Rosey laughed when I told him about it, and how Roger Staubach laughed when Chris called him Roger Starbuckle. I remembered too how Barry Sanders said he wanted to find out who he was apart from football—the person God had created him to be.

Maybe that's what I needed to concentrate on as well. Maybe it didn't matter if people got my name wrong or didn't even know or care what it was. God knew—and He cared. And when all the autographing parties and award ceremonies had passed away and only our service to our Lord remained, what would matter then?

Humbled as I was after those experiences, I was encouraged too. I was through crawling and walking and even running; I was soaring now, flying with the eagles. So what if I still did an occasional face-plant? If that's what it took to keep things in perspective, then I'd accept it. God had called me and gifted me, and I was going to pursue whatever He had for me. Life was just too exciting to live it on the sidelines. Face-plants notwithstanding, I couldn't wait to see what else God had in store for me.

I redoubled my efforts. I wrote more, read more, prayed more, got more involved in church, branched out in ministry....

Then, in the midst of this swirl of excitement and frenzy of activity, I found myself being drawn into an entirely new area of ministry—one I would never have imagined. Had anyone told me I would get involved in it, I would have vehemently denied it. I had no interest, no experience, and seemingly nothing to offer.

Little did I know that I was about to see humility and discipleship in action, and experience a series of events that would take me from my soaring position back to my knees—once and for all.

Making It Personal

Have you ever found yourself in a position where you expected to receive a great honor, only to be humbled and brought back to reality in one swift motion? How did you react? What do you learn from it? How has it changed your life and impacted the lives of others?

"For whoever exalts himself will be abased, and he who humbles himself will be exalted."
—Luke 14:11

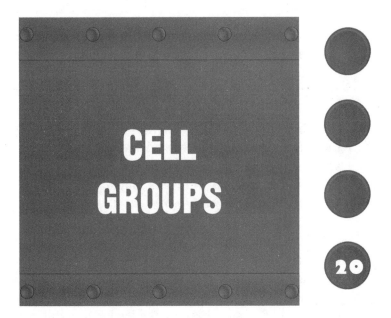

CELL
GROUPS

It started with a simple two-line blurb in the church bulletin, one I scarcely noticed and would have ignored even if it had been printed in giant, bold-faced type: "Anyone interested in becoming involved in jail ministry, please meet in the conference room on Tuesday evening at 7 P.M." It was the type of generic announcement that fills space in the bulletins of many churches, and which receives little or no response. Besides, I had other things going on that evening....

Promptly at 6:30 on Tuesday evening I pulled into the church parking lot, surprised that I was the first to arrive for the women's ministry meeting. This was the sort of thing that usually generated a good turnout, particularly when we were planning for our annual retreat. Wise and experienced women's ministry leaders—myself included—had long since learned that if you wanted one of the choice assignments on the planning committee (i.e., greeting/hobnobbing with the guest speaker), as opposed to one of the leftover jobs that get assigned to the no-shows (setting up chairs or copying/folding program brochures), get to the meeting early. It seemed my plum assignment was assured.

It was nearly seven when the first couple of cars pulled into the lot, followed a few minutes later by three more. Strangely, I noticed that two of the drivers were men, and the other three were ladies I'd never seen at women's ministry meetings before, though I did recognize all of them from other church-related functions. I watched them go inside, waited five more minutes, and when no one else arrived, I went in to see what was going on. Maybe I had the time wrong, though I doubted it, since all women's ministry meetings started at 6:30, and it was now a few minutes after seven.

I made my way straight to the fellowship hall, only to find it dark and uninhabited. When I flipped on the lights, I noticed the sign on the wall next to the doorway: "Women's Ministry Planning Meeting, Fellowship Hall, Thursday, 6:30 P.M."

Then I remembered. Last time, we'd voted to move this meeting to Thursday because the leader couldn't be there on Tuesday.

Once again my overly busy schedule had caused me to forget something. It seemed to be happening a lot lately, but I supposed it couldn't be helped. I simply had so many things to keep track of that it was impossible to remember everything.

At the same time, I had to admit that a reminder of the change of meeting nights had probably been printed in Sunday's bulletin. I, as usual, hadn't bothered to read it closely enough, and now, here I was, all dressed up and nowhere to go.

As I made my way back down the hall toward the exit, I passed the conference room, where voices lifted in prayer drifted out to me from behind the closed door. I took another step, telling myself that whatever meeting was going on in that room had nothing to do with me, but my feet suddenly felt cemented to the floor. The longer I stood there, the more my heart was drawn to open the door and join in, and the more sure I was that I hadn't come to church that night by accident after all.

I opened the door as quietly as possible and peeked inside. The three ladies and two men I'd seen pulling into the parking lot earlier now stood in a circle, hands joined and heads bowed, calling out to God for wisdom and direction—and for workers to enter the harvest fields.

That sounded very much like something that could suck away even more time from my already overloaded calendar. I tried to turn and walk away, but an invisible hand held me in place. My heart began to race and tears came to my eyes, as I argued silently: *God, you know I can't sign up for anything else! I'm too busy already.*

Though I heard no voice, I sensed a wholehearted agreement to my "I'm too busy already" statement. Why, then, would God want me to get involved in something else?

As I stood there, caught between obedience and running for my life, the group of prayer warriors broke rank and noticed me standing there. Sally, the lady who seemed to be heading the group, flashed a warm smile and called, "Kathi, come on in! We're so glad you decided to join us."

Before I could explain that I hadn't made any sort of decision and wasn't even sure what they were doing, Sally looped her arm through mine and steered me over to their small circle. "Look who's here," she announced, as the rest of the group joined in her hearty welcome.

Before the evening was over I'd agreed to join them on their next outing to the Youth Authority, a coed prison for offenders ranging in age from preteen to early 20s, convicted of crimes ranging from drug possession to rape and murder. What was I thinking?

Challenged Behind Bars

Though I'll admit I was shaking in my boots when I made my first trek behind bars and mingled with a group of youthful inmates, many with gang tattoos decorating nearly every uncovered inch of their bodies, I was hooked. From the moment I sat down to talk with a young woman named

Camille, who'd just turned 17 and had been locked up for three years for murdering her pimp, I knew I'd never be the same. When I prayed with a 14-year-old boy named Richard, convicted of selling drugs to elementary-aged children—at the insistence of his drug-addicted mother—I knew I couldn't walk away. I'd found a niche, and I'd have to work out the time details one way or another.

Then, after several months of involvement in this particular ministry, I had a call from a national prison ministry, asking if I'd accompany them on a few of their prison ministry weekends, during which they went into prisons all across the country. They hoped I'd consider writing a book about the revival that was going on in the bleak setting of the prison system. Once again I argued with myself over agreeing to such an invitation, and once again I found myself compelled to get involved.

The next thing I knew I was sitting in a chapel in Huntsville State Prison in Texas, meeting with inmates who'd once been considered some of the most dangerous in their state and who were now serving as chaplain's assistants, discipling the ever-burgeoning numbers of new converts under their oversight. I was amazed at their level of commitment, but even more so at their level of humility. Not one of them proclaimed his innocence or insisted on his right to be released from prison now that he'd become a Christian. Instead, each one proclaimed his thankfulness that God had saved him and given him the privilege of serving Him behind bars.

No one better epitomized this humble servant attitude than a man named Bill, whom I met on a one-day visit to San Quentin's infamous death row (California). Bill had been convicted of rape and murder more than a decade earlier and, at the time of my visit, had the longest unheard appeal in the state. It was obvious, as I spoke and prayed with Bill and watched him interact with the other prisoners and even the correctional officers, that God was prolonging Bill's life for a reason.

Bill related to me that he'd received Jesus as his Lord and Savior through the ministry of a jail chaplain. Bill had been arrested and was awaiting trial when this devoted chaplain visited him and led him to the Lord. Though God's gracious salvation assured Bill of forgiveness for all his sins and eternal life now and forever, it didn't erase his sinful actions or their penalties. Bill was convicted and sentenced to death, then sent to prison to await his execution.

When he arrived there he cried out to God and said, "Lord, You know I'm a new believer and I need fellowship so I can grow. How is that going to happen here? I need to be with other Christians. Please, if I have to be here, send other Christians here too!"

He had no sooner prayed that prayer than he realized how selfish it was. Why would he want God to send other Christians to death row? He immediately repented and asked God to help him be a godly witness to others who were already there and to help them come to know the Lord.

God answered that second prayer without hesitation. In a matter of weeks, Bill was not only leading other prisoners to Christ, but correctional officers as well. As the number of believers on death row grew, they began to meet together in one another's cells for prayer and Bible study.

"We give an entirely new meaning to the term 'cell groups,'" Bill joked. "And our numbers are still growing. Even some of the guards join us when they can. Our goal is to reach every man on the row so not one will go to the chamber without Jesus in his heart."

I've never forgotten that statement. Though I've long since lost touch with Bill and many of the other inmates I've met through the years, Bill's words continue to call me to a deeper level of commitment. Bill said something else to me that day that God seared into my brain, though I didn't understand at the time what I could do about it or how to remedy the situation. When I mentioned the many ministries I was involved with and all the other obligations I had, he asked, "How do you do it?" Then, after a pause, he asked, "*Why* do you do it?"

His first question stumped me; the second one silenced me. I had no answer for either of them, but the *why* question was like a knife in my heart. Wasn't I doing all I was doing because I was a Christian? Because I was a woman who wanted to emulate the dedication and achievement of the Proverbs 31 woman? Because the time was short and I wanted to make a difference before I left this earth?

It was no wonder I had no answer for Bill, since I had none for myself. A man on death row, convicted of rape and murder, yet saved and redeemed by the blood of Jesus, had posed a question that would haunt me every step of the way from my exit through the San Quentin gates... and back into my everyday life. God had called me to prison ministry; I was sure of that. But why? So I could minister to the prisoners— or so they could minister to me?

And what about all those other things I was doing—family, classes at church, ministry involvement? All good things, but were they all necessary things? It was obvious that God had called me to my commitment to my family, but had He called me to everything else, or had I signed up on my own?

I didn't have any answers yet, but thanks to a man on death row, I intended to find out.

 Making It Personal

Have you ever found yourself challenged on some very personal issues by an unlikely or unexpected source? Was there validity in the challenge? If so, how did you react? How has your life—or someone else's—been changed as a result?

Remember the prisoners as if chained with them.
—Hebrews 13:3

Learning to Lean— Back on My Knees

I will boast all the more gladly about my weaknesses, so that Christ's power may rest on me.... For when I am weak, then I am strong.
—2 Corinthians 12:9–10 (NIV)

Weary, Heavy-Laden, and Ready to Rest

I was tired. Exhausted. Worn out. And I'd come to the conclusion that all this learning to crawl and walk and run stuff is for the birds. Oh, wait. Sorry. It's the flying part that's for the birds, isn't it? The truth is that I'd used up just about every ounce of strength and energy I had making my way through those four stages of spiritual growth, and now I was sorely tempted to give it all up. The only reason I didn't was...what's the alternative? I felt like Peter when Jesus asked him if he was going to desert Him. The frustrated but honest disciple answered, "Where would I go, Lord? You have the words of life." (See John 6:68.)

Exactly. Jesus had the words of life, and I had Jesus. There was nowhere else to go. He was everything—my Savior, my Lord, my only hope. I knew that. I believed it with everything in me. I had no doubt He was exactly who He said He was: the Way, the Truth, and the Life. (See John 14:6.) I had no problem with His claims of being the only Way to the Father and the complete embodiment of all Truth. So why was I stumbling over His claim of being "the Life." Mentally, I was OK with that statement. The problem was in my heart. I didn't *feel* His Life in me, though I knew it was there. The only thing I felt was weary and heavy-laden.

"I'm tired, Lord," I said one morning, as I sat on the edge of my bed facing yet another long day. "I need to rest."

I know. But are you ready?

I was too surprised and confused to answer. What was God asking me? Was I ready? Ready for what? Ready for a new direction in ministry? Ready for some new assignment?

Are you ready to rest?

Of course I was ready to rest! Didn't I just say...?

You said you needed to rest. I know that. You've needed to rest for a long time. I'm asking if you're ready.

My heart stopped, as Jesus's words from Matthew 11:28 echoed in my mind: "Come to Me, all you who labor and are heavy laden, and I will give you rest." How many times had I read that verse? And why had I never paid attention?

I slipped from my bed and sprawled on the floor, listening....

Peace. Be still.

I couldn't have moved if I'd wanted to.

Be still, and know that I am God.

I thought I'd known that for many years, but now it came

as revelation, as if I were hearing it for the very first time. Maybe it was because I was finally being still. And I stayed that way for a very long time, soaking up the remarkable, life-changing truth that God is God, and nothing else mattered.

It was several hours before I rose from my prone position, feeling as if I'd just returned from a long and restful vacation. I had a seemingly never-ending list of things to do that day, and I'd done none of them. A mere 24 hours earlier I would have been in a panic over my lack of accomplishment. This day I was completely at peace, knowing I'd done the only thing I truly needed to do—rest. I'd finally obeyed Jesus's command to come to Him and rest, to be still and know that He is God... not me.

What a lesson! I felt like I'd learned more in those few hours of resting *in Him* than in all the previous years of trying to do things *for Him*. And I'd learned it right back where I first started as a spiritual rug rat—on my knees. I smiled, realizing I'd come full circle. Only this time I had no desire to get up off my knees and learn to walk or run or fly. I just wanted to be still and listen for His voice, to know that He is God and that all else will one day pass away.

I was finally ready to rest.

GONE OFF THE DEEP END

21

Never one to do something halfway, I quickly took resting to an entirely new level. No more tight ships for me! I had cannons rolling around everywhere, and I didn't care. I'd resigned my membership in the "Martha Club" and fully intended to spend the rest of my life sitting at Jesus's feet, right next to Martha's much wiser and exceedingly more spiritual sister, Mary.

Mundane chores like fixing dinner, doing laundry, or returning phone calls weren't even blips on my radar screen. After years of frantic activity, I was completely dedicated to resting, and I had no intention of allowing anything to distract me.

This went on for several days. Then, one morning, I was rudely interrupted by 15 minutes of nonstop doorbell ringing, fist-pounding, and threats to call the police if I didn't respond. Finally I decided I'd better set my Bible and prayer journal aside long enough to diffuse the situation.

I knew it was Linda out there, the one who'd convinced me to join a gym and to go public to boost my book sales. In all fairness, the going public part had turned out to be a relatively successful idea. But that was before I discovered God wanted me to rest, to sit at His feet and learn about Him, to lean against His chest like the Apostle John at the Last Supper and listen to Jesus's heartbeat. Besides, didn't the Bible say that promotion comes only from God? I'd finally realized that if I dedicated myself to spending time with God, I could just sit back and let Him take care of everything else, including my book sales. And that's exactly what I intended to do.

Linda was still pounding and ringing and hollering when I got to the door, and apparently making a futile attempt to peer the wrong way through the peep hole as well, because as soon as I yanked the door open she tumbled inside and nearly knocked me over. I managed not to laugh, but the look on her face as the door flew open and she made a completely unexpected and less than graceful entrance was something I won't forget any time soon.

"How have you been?" I asked, helping her to her feet.

She looked at me as if I were the one who'd just popped in from another planet. "How have *I* been?" Her wide eyes blinked in disbelief, but for the life of me I couldn't imagine why. Then she repeated herself, raising her voice an octave or two. "How have *I* been? I can't believe you asked me that. Shouldn't the question be, how have *you* been? Better yet, *where* have you been? You're the one who didn't show up for women's Bible study yesterday morning and didn't answer the phone when I called—12 times, I might add."

I was beginning to get the distinct impression that she was unhappy with me for some reason. "You sound upset," I observed.

I hadn't thought it possible, but her already saucer-sized eyes opened even wider. Her mouth moved, and I thought she was going to say something, but then she shook her head and sighed. "Can we sit down? I really don't feel like having this conversation here in the entryway."

This conversation? What conversation? Did I miss something? I decided to wait until we sat down before I asked.

No sense agitating her anymore than she already was, though I still had no idea what had upset her in the first place.

I led the way into the living room, where we plunked down on opposite ends of the couch, facing each other. From the corner of my eye I saw my Bible and prayer journal waiting patiently for me on the coffee table, but I disciplined myself to focus on my friend, who was obviously in some sort of distress.

"Would you like some coffee?" I asked. "Or maybe a soda or a glass of water?"

"I'm not thirsty, thanks," she answered, her voice flat—a sure sign she was trying to control her emotions. Whatever was bothering her, it was big.

"Cookies?" I offered. "I have no idea what kind they are, but I'm sure there are a few left in the cupboard."

Linda lifted her eyes to mine and locked on as if she had her own private heat-seeking missile. "I'm not thirsty, and I'm not hungry," she said, her teeth clenched as she spoke.

Wow, she really was freaking out over something. I shot up a quick prayer that God would give me insight into how to answer her once she voiced her problem. Chances are she just needed to learn a bit more about resting....

Her eyes narrowed, and her forehead drew together. "You really don't know why I'm here, do you?"

Experience had taught me that that kind of question implied I should know the answer. But I didn't. "I'm sorry, but no, I don't have a clue why you're here or why you seem to be upset."

Back on Track

Linda's eyebrows shot up. "*Seem* to be upset! Well, you're right about that. I most definitely am upset, and that's why I'm here. I'm trying to find out what happened to you yesterday."

"Yesterday?"

The expression on her face indicated imminent meltdown.

When the smoke seeping out of her ears finally cleared, she hissed, "Yes. Yesterday. Women's Bible study. Remember?"

I shrugged. Sure, I remembered. I also remembered that Linda was the one who led the study, but I'd never seen her so riled over someone missing one time. What was the big deal anyway? I mean, where was it written in blood that I had to attend every single class or be subjected to an irate grilling, from someone I thought was my friend? Something told me to cool my flippant attitude before I answered.

So, calmly I replied, "I do remember there was a study yesterday, sure. But I'm afraid I don't see—"

"You remember there was a study yesterday," Linda interrupted. "Obviously you don't remember that you agreed to lead that study so I could drive my mother to her doctor's appointment."

Oops! It was all starting to come back to me. Linda's mom, the doctor's appointment, the class. She was right. I had agreed to take over for her. But that was last week, before I began spending more quality time with the Lord. I hated to admit it, but my promise to her had completely slipped my mind. In fact, I hadn't thought of the Bible study at all until now.

"I'm so sorry," I said, meaning every word. "You know I don't make promises I don't intend to keep. It's just...I totally forgot about it. I've been so—"

"Busy?" Linda said, finishing my sentence. "What else is new? You're always busy. That's never stopped you before. You're the one person I thought I could count on to keep her word. That's why I've been so worried. Ever since I got home yesterday and heard the message on my answering machine from Barbara, saying she had to take over the class at the last minute because you didn't show, I've been worried sick about you."

I felt the heat rush to my cheeks, as I realized I owed an apology to more than just Linda. "Oh, no, I'm so sorry about the class! Poor Barbara..."

"It's not the class Barbara and I were worried about." Linda was still frowning, but it looked more like concern than anger now. "They managed just fine without us. God showed up, proving you and I are not indispensable. But Barbara and I couldn't imagine what happened to you. Why do you think I kept calling? Didn't you hear the phone? Didn't you check your messages?"

I did vaguely remember hearing the phone ringing off and on throughout the day yesterday, and this morning too. But I'd decided I wasn't going to let anything distract me from the peace and joy I'd found in my deepened relationship with Jesus. Surely Linda would understand that.

"I've been spending time with God," I explained. "Lots of time, actually. As much as possible. Just a few days ago I realized how much time I've spent doing things *for* God and how little time I've actually spent *with* Him, you know what I mean? Resting in Him. It's wonderful. So wonderful I don't want to do anything else. I feel like I've finally graduated from being a Martha, running around in 90 directions and grumbling about how busy I am. Now I just want to be like Mary, sitting at Jesus's feet and listening to Him."

When Linda didn't respond right away, I felt myself getting defensive. "Jesus commended her for that, you know."

My friend nodded. "I know. And you're right. Sitting at Jesus' feet and listening to Him is a wonderful thing, probably the most important thing any of us will ever do. But that doesn't mean we don't do anything else. We have responsibilities, you know. Families, friends, jobs...commitments."

That last word hung in the air like an accusing, condemning cloud, waiting to descend and dump cold water all over me. She was right. I couldn't stop living so I could sit and read the Bible and pray all day. But I didn't want to get sucked back into the spin cycle of life either. *There has to be a balance,* I thought.

Linda reached over and laid her hand on mine. When she spoke, her words went straight to my heart. "The Bible says we're to seek God and His kingdom *first*, and what you're doing is a good thing—a really good thing. But the Bible also says we're to 'occupy' or 'do business' until He comes. God wants us to spend time with Him, to put Him first, to be willing to die for Him if need be. But He also knows we have to perform the daily functions of life. One of the last things Jesus did before He returned to heaven after the Resurrection was to command His followers to go into all the world and make disciples. The first step in making disciples is to sit at Jesus's feet and learn from Him. But then we have to get up and go."

Once again, I'd lost my balance. This time, instead of getting so busy working for God that I forgot to spend time with Him, I'd become so wrapped up in the sweet fellowship of resting in His presence that I'd forgotten there was a lost and hurting world out there that needed to hear about His rest too.

Would I never learn? How long was this painful growing and learning process going to continue?

Until you come home to be with Me.

I smiled, His words a gentle reminder that I was still His work in progress.

Linda smiled too. "Forgive me. I didn't mean to come down on you so hard. I was just—"

"Concerned," I said, and nodded. "I know. And thank you for caring."

This time it was God's smile I sensed filling the room, as two of His children took another step closer to Him—and to one another. *Love Me with all your heart, soul, and strength,* He reminded me. *Only then can you begin to love others as you love yourself. Then you will truly find My rest.*

 **Making It Personal**

Have there been times in your life when you struggled to find the right balance between resting and doing? How did spending time with God's Word and His people help you achieve that balance? When was the last time you took time to rest? Are there other times when you forget the "going" aspect of the Christian life?

● ● ● ● ●

"Come to Me, all you who labor and are heavy laden, and I will give you rest."
—Matthew 11:28

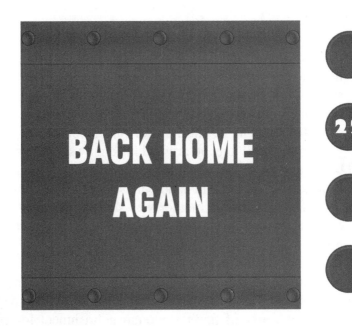

BACK HOME AGAIN

22

My dad was born in Germany just prior to World War I, and he quickly learned of the hardships of growing up in a country at war. His mother—my grandmother, whose name was Jenny and whom we lovingly called "Omi"—was a Christian, though she had little teaching or training in the Scriptures. Still, she taught her children what she knew, and she prayed for them faithfully. Though my dad, whose name was Hans, somehow lost his way and rejected her teachings, her prayers stayed hot on his heels. Here is his story—and how it became an integral part of my own, particularly as it applied to my "resting in Him and His faithfulness" stage.

Hans was a quiet boy—not by nature, but by circumstance. It wasn't easy being a five-year-old when there was a war going on. His father was away in the Kaiser's army, his brother had succumbed to malnutrition, and now it was just him and his mother, Jenny. Two hungry souls in a sea of suffering humanity, waiting in line after endless line for their daily ration of rutabaga soup and dry bread; if all went well, there would be enough soup for their evening meal. If not, they would go to bed hungry...again.

And yet, even if Hans had to lie in bed at night and listen to his stomach growl, he knew there would be another sound—a welcome, comforting sound—to drown out his complaining stomach. His mother's singing; he never tired of it. One day, as he shuffled forward a couple of steps in yet another food line, he gripped his empty soup bowl in his hands and looked up at her. She smiled at him, warming his heart as she laid her thin hand on his shoulder. Hans was old enough to realize his mother was short compared to most other adults, but he was still young enough to have to crane his neck to see her beautiful face.

She was a beauty, his mother, despite the pain of having been orphaned at an early age, losing a child, and wondering whether her husband was dead or alive. Beautiful, despite the daily worry of finding enough nourishment for Hans, regardless of whether or not she ate anything herself—which she often didn't, as she shared her own meager portions with her remaining son. Hans had heard Jenny's stomach growl louder than his own many times, even as she sang him to sleep at night.

The young boy with the dark hair and sky-blue eyes returned his mother's smile, in spite of the pain in his stomach and the ache of his cold feet, which were crammed into the cardboard-soled shoes he had worn for two winters now. Shivering in the frigid wind that howled off the river and pierced his threadbare jacket, Hans marveled at his mother's strength. Didn't she feel the cold as he did? Or the hunger? If she did, she never said anything, only smiled her reassuring smile and went on with whatever needed to be done.

How Hans loved the comforting familiarity of his mother's face. He scarcely could recall his father, who had been gone for more than two years now, or even his brother, who had died a year earlier. It was his mother's voice that kept him going, singing to him at night, soothing him, encouraging him, offering him hope where there was no hope. Things would get better, her songs seemed to promise, if not today, then soon...some day...whether in this life or in the next. God watched over them, the songs proclaimed; He loved them, and He would never, ever leave them. Hans clung to the words of his mother's songs, even as the war dragged on, day after miserable, endless day. Better times were coming, the lyrics assured him. He had only to wait, and God would bring them to pass.

And so he waited. Through the ever-growing food lines and the ever-shrinking food rations; the bleak, dreary, freezing winters; the lonely, seemingly interminable vigil, shared only with his mother, as they watched and wondered if Hans's father would ever return; the long weeks in an impersonal, government-run hospital as the frightened, lonely little boy lay on his back, being treated for scurvy while his mother sat at his side, praying and singing.

Then, finally, it was over. The war ended, and Hans's father came home. But life in post-World War I Germany was still very hard. A sister and two brothers were soon added to the family. As the eldest child, Hans had to grow up quickly, accept responsibility, and get on with taking care of himself. By the time he was 18, he had left home, traveling alone from Germany to America, where he hoped to make his fortune and finally realize those better days his mother's songs had promised.

As the long and difficult ocean voyage drew to a close and the stifling, overcrowded ship steamed past the Statue of Liberty, her arm raised in welcome, Hans prepared to arrive in the "promised land"—just in time for the Great Depression. Rather than better days, he once again found himself fighting for survival. Only this time his mother wasn't there to sing him to sleep. This time, with few skills and only rudimentary English, he was alone in his hardships, with no one to ease the pain and fear that threatened to envelop him. Soon his childlike heart became hardened, the soothing, faith-building songs of his boyhood forgotten as cynicism set in and he learned to rely only on himself.

After one failed marriage, producing two sons he seldom saw, he married again and raised three more children, working two jobs most of his life in order to give his loved ones what he himself had lacked as a boy. In addition, after faithfully serving his new homeland in World War II, he managed to scrape together enough money to bring the remainder of his family from Germany to America, so they too might start a new life. But each time his by then widowed mother, or his wife and children—and even his grandchildren—attempted to speak to him of God's love, he would have none of it. If there was a God at all, he argued, the Almighty cared nothing for him; therefore, he would return the lack of caring and go on with his life without any help from this God or His empty promises.

Answered Prayer

And go on he did, retiring at last to raise Christmas trees on a small farm in the rainy Washington State countryside. He continued to reject talk of a loving God—until finally his hair turned gray and his step slowed, his back stooped, and his eyes dimmed. That's when the voices started, strange yet familiar voices that he simply could not reason away. Still, though he heard the voices singing, calling to him from the past—or were they calling him into the future?—he refused to believe. Time and circumstances had taught him the futility of belief in anything he couldn't see or touch. An aberration, he reasoned, a sign of advancing age. There was no other logical explanation for the sweet voices he heard from time to time, voices that tugged at the long-buried memories of his heart as they sang their German hymns of faith and promise.

Once, he confided in his grown daughter about the voices. She, by then a Christian, suggested they were angels, singing to him of God's love and urging him to believe. But he rejected her explanation, and never mentioned the voices again.

Then it happened. Cancer. Heart failure. Hardening of the arteries. A series of ministrokes. It was just past his 88th birthday, but Hans was beginning to regress—first, to his working days before he retired; then, back to the time when his children were young; and even before that, to his early days as a young man in America, struggling to find his way in the world. Finally, his English became blurred with German, the native language he had seldom spoken for decades. The weakened old man with the trembling hands, spindly legs, and clouded eyes had returned to his childhood. And in that childhood, he began to sing—sometimes in German, sometimes in English—of a time long ago, a land far away, and a faith almost forgotten. Amidst the ancient hymns, "Jesus loves me, this I know," sprang from his withered, cracked lips, as Hans crooned to his grateful family, who listened and watched, their eyes filled with tears. The grandfather, the father, the husband had once again become a child, and in the memories of his childhood he had found the simplicity to believe.

Jesus said: "Unless you change and become like little children, you will never enter the kingdom of heaven" (Matthew 18:3 NIV). Hans could not come as a man—his heart had grown too hard. But he came as a child, and he did indeed see God's kingdom, shining from the heavens, beckoning him with angel voices to come home.

On October 23, 1999, with his family gathered around his bedside at his beloved tree farm in Washington, the little boy named Hans slipped out of his "old man" suit, smiled a final farewell to his loved ones, and was reunited with his mother as, together, they joined in singing with the angels. A mother's faith, the prayers of loved ones, and most of all the mercy of God had brought yet another child home.

Yes, I was that grown daughter in whom my father, Hans, confided about the voices he heard, singing the old German hymns his mother—my grandmother—had taught him so many years before. I was that grown daughter who sat at his side during one of his last days on this earth, just before another stroke took his ability to speak clearly, and heard him sing in his little-boy voice, "Jesus loves me."

It was a time no one in my family will ever forget. How long we'd prayed for this precious but stubborn man to receive Jesus as his Savior! And how long he'd refused to listen! Though we loved him dearly, our memories of Dad up until that last week were of his hard-working yet headstrong ways—and of the sometimes hilarious moments that resulted from them.

My youngest brother, Jerry, will never forget the time he drove Dad to pick up his riding mower from the repair shop. After the mechanic had loaded it into the back of Dad's truck and tied it down, Dad decided they shouldn't leave the parking lot until they were sure it ran. (Why he didn't do that *before* loading it into the truck is anyone's guess!) And so, right there in the middle of a very busy parking lot—on a very wet and rainy southwest Washington day—my poor brother had to climb up into the bed of Dad's truck and onto the mower, then start the engine so Dad could hear it run and be satisfied that it had been fixed properly.

Dad saw nothing unusual about his request, while Jerry was mortified—yet not surprised. That was simply the way Dad did things. To this day, we laugh about so many of those instances (though we often didn't laugh then).

But thanks to God's faithfulness—and a mother's prayers—we also have beautiful memories of our precious father singing of Jesus's love for him. The experience taught me so much about resting and trusting in God's goodness to His children. And in those first few days after Dad graduated to heaven, I found myself thinking more and more of Omi and wondering—was she the Proverbs 31 role model I'd been seeking for so many years?

 **Making It Personal**

What watershed experiences have taken place in your life that pulled things into perspective for you? What did you learn from those times, and how are you changed because of them? Can you think of a time when you saw God answer your prayers but only after many, many years?

● ● ● ● ●

So God heard their groaning, and God remembered His covenant with Abraham, with Isaac, and with Jacob.
—Exodus 2:24

BERNADINE
RETURNS

23

Several years had passed since I'd had any contact with Bernadine. When we first started to lose touch, I was bothered, especially when I realized I hadn't seen her at Bible study or worship services for quite some time. But after awhile, as much as I hate to admit it, I got caught up in the busyness of life and forgot about her.

Then one morning, not long after the Lord began teaching me how to rest in Him and about the same time my dad had "graduated" to sing with the angels, Bernadine rang my doorbell. I'd been thinking a lot about my grandmother during those weeks following my dad's home-going, and I'd come to the conclusion that Omi really was a good Proverbs 31 role model, even though she was no longer around to mentor me. I realized she successfully modeled the part of a godly woman through her teachings to her children when they were little, praying for them for as long as she was on this earth, and leaving the rest to God. She'd done her part, and learned to rest in her Savior. I would do well to do the same.

That's where I was when Bernadine showed up. She hadn't changed much since I'd last seen her, but her smile was gone, and that bothered me more than anything.

"How are you?" I asked, motioning her inside and cringing with guilt as I remembered how I'd hidden from her in times past—until my son called me on it. I cringed even more when I realized I'd abandoned her over the years, never even following up with a phone call when she dropped out of sight. Was that any way to treat your spiritual "baby"?

"I'm OK," she answered, her voice lacking its usual *joie de vivre* as I escorted her into the kitchen. When I offered her a cold drink, she shrugged and answered, "Sure, whatever," and sank into a kitchen chair. I felt a pang of guilt and reasoned that whatever was bothering my friend was obviously my fault. *If I'd just been there for her—*

Stop it, I told myself. *This is not about you; it's about Bernadine and her relationship with God. Just rest in the Lord, and let Him use you.*

"Let's go with iced tea," I said, trying to coax a smile from the downcast woman, "especially since that's all I've got."

She forced an obligatory smile but said nothing as I plunked ice cubes into the glasses. By the time I joined her, there were tears in her eyes.

"What have I done?" she asked, shaking her head. "You introduced me to Jesus, and He gave me a wonderful new life. Then . . . I threw it all away." Her shoulders shook and the sobs came, and I found myself sitting across from her, two glasses of untouched iced tea between us, watching her cry while I felt as useless as a pair of roller skates at a mermaid convention.

Finally I had the good sense to move my chair next to hers and put an arm around her shoulders. I kept thinking I should say something brilliant and profound, something to make her pain go away and bring back the jolly, upbeat Bernadine I used to know and . . . well, sort of love. But then I knew God was telling me to keep my mouth shut and just sit there with her and let her cry—maybe even cry a little with her—and wait until she was ready to talk.

That was harder than spouting platitudes. Everything in me wanted to say things like, "Don't cry, Bernadine. We all blow it sometimes. God knows. He understands, and He still loves you. It's going to be all right, honest."

All those things were true, but I realized I didn't want to say them so much for Bernadine as for myself. I didn't like feeling helpless and useless, sitting there with my arm around Bernadine and letting her hurt instead of trying to fix her. Superwoman would have fixed her; she would have found a way. But if I'd learned anything through the years and decades since I first aspired to fly through the air and rescue the world it was that I most definitely was not Superwoman. I wasn't the Proverbs 31 woman either, so maybe it was best to keep my big mouth shut and not risk sticking my foot in it, as I'd been known to do countless times in the past.

And so I sat, mouth clamped shut and arm around Bernadine's shoulder, patting her as comfortingly as I could but saying nothing. Finally her sobs turned to occasional sniffles and hiccups, as she availed herself of the box of tissues I'd had the foresight to place in front of her just before moving my chair next to hers.

Full Circle

"How do you always know the right thing to say and do?" she asked. "I wish I was like you. You're so wise and mature."

I felt my eyes widen until I thought they'd pop out of their sockets. Wise and mature? Always knowing the right thing to say and do? I was beginning to wonder if Bernadine had stopped by to confess that she was using hallucinogenic drugs. It was definitely time for me to jump in and clear up her misconceptions.

"Bernadine, I—"

That was as far as I got, as she held up her hand to cut me off. "I know what you're going to say, and you're right.

I walked away from church, from fellowship with other believers, from everything you and others taught me—all because I thought I was 'in love.'" She shook her head. "No one had ever paid attention to me that way before, and...when I met Dan and he kept telling me how beautiful I was..."

I was afraid she was going to erupt in tears again, so I moved the tissue box closer, but she managed to pull herself together and continue. "I wanted to believe him, even though I knew it wasn't true. It was just...so nice to get all that attention, to have someone call me and pay attention to me, to be the center of someone's world." She shrugged again. "I don't know if you can understand, because you've always been beautiful and popular...."

Now I was sure she was on drugs, but I continued to keep my mouth closed and my heart and ears open, wondering when God was going to give me something wise and mature to say or do, since I sure didn't have anything of my own to contribute.

"Anyway," she said, taking a deep breath and looking into my eyes, "like I said, I know what you're thinking, and you're right. I sinned, and I need to repent. That's why I'm here. I need you to pray with me and counsel me and tell me what to do to get back on track with God. I know the Bible says that if I confess my sins, He'll forgive me, but I need to hear that from someone else—someone I respect, like you. I need to know that God will forgive me—and that you and others will too."

She took another deep breath and waited, staring at me as if her entire future hinged on my reaction. I knew it didn't, but I'd never felt more inept in my entire life.

"Bernadine, of course God will forgive you. He already has. He sent His Son to pay the price for your sins—and mine. All of them—past, present, and future. He's never stopped loving you. He wants you back in His arms, safe and sound, where you belong."

Where did that come from, I wondered. It sounded wise and mature, so it had to be God, not me. What a relief! This resting in God stuff really worked. I opened my mouth and trusted God to keep talking.

"And who am I—or anyone else—not to forgive you? If Jesus hadn't died for my sins, I'd never make it through a day without being condemned to hell. I'd be doomed in five minutes. The fact that you think I'm wise and mature is absolutely amazing. Bernadine, I'm no different than you. I need Jesus every day—every minute—and even then I fall flat on my face half the time."

I smiled and laid my hand on her arm. "All that matters is that your Father has called you back to His heart, and you answered the call. Are you ready to pray now, to ask God to forgive and restore you? I'll be glad to pray with you."

She nodded. "I'd like that. And I was right. You are wise and mature. You didn't say anything while I was crying; you just held me and let me get it all out until I was ready to talk. Then you listened. Do you know how rare that is? That has to be God in you. Isn't that where wisdom and maturity come from?"

I smiled. Bernadine may have strayed away for a while, but she'd be back on track and growing in the Lord in no time. She had the basics pegged: God living in us, and us resting in Him; that's what wisdom and maturity are all about. Omi knew it. My mom knew it. Betty and Ruth and Cora knew it. Marcy and Linda and Luci knew it. My nephew Larson and granddaughter Brittney seemed to understand it to some degree. Mara and her mother certainly knew it. Maybe Imogene had even figured it out somewhere along the line. Football great Barry Sanders and the members of the San Quentin Death Row cell groups definitely knew it. And my precious father had learned it in his last days on earth. Now I was finally figuring it out. It was obvious it wouldn't take Bernadine long; in fact, it seemed she was several steps ahead of me on that front already.

As Bernadine and I joined hands and prepared to spend time with our Father, my longtime friend and former "pest" looked at me and said, "Kathi, do you think you could find time in your schedule to mentor me, to be a role model to help me grow in my walk with the Lord? I want to be a serious disciple—like you—and I think you'd be the perfect mentor for me. You remind me so much of the Proverbs 31 woman, and I'd like to model my life after hers. I know it's a lot to ask, but I'd appreciate it if you'd consider doing that for me."

I couldn't get any words past the lump in my throat, as Bernadine's face blurred through the tears that stung my eyes. *Oh, God, You are beyond amazing! How is it possible that you could take someone like me, who wouldn't know the Proverbs 31 woman if I tripped over her—and often did!—and use me to inspire and mentor someone else? Oh, Lord, be my strength, my wisdom, my maturity, for I have nothing to offer on my own.*

In that moment I was sure I could see God smile, as He assured me my prayer would be answered, as it was just the type of prayer He longed to hear His children pray.

Making It Personal

What experiences in your life have brought you full circle in some area of spiritual maturity and growth? How did you feel when you first realized what God was doing and how He was using you and your experiences to minister to others?

If we confess our sins, He is faithful and just to forgive us our sins and to cleanse us from all unrighteousness.
—1 John 1:9

"SOMEBODY HAS TO SET UP THE CHAIRS"

24

I'm one of those people who tends to stick my fingers in my ears and chant, "La la la la la," when someone says something I don't want to hear. When the Someone who's saying it is God, that's not a good thing.

I've known that for years, but it really hit home with me at the end of 2005. As I often do when a new year approaches, I was spending a little extra time alone with God, seeking His direction for the coming year. I was still learning what it means to rest in God, and at least Bernadine thought I was on my way to finally earning Proverbs 31 woman status. It seemed obvious to me then, since I'd finally had some spiritual breakthroughs, that I must be on the verge of other great breakthroughs. Though my previously published books had experienced some level of success through the years and God had used me to speak and minister in various venues and situations, I hadn't achieved superstar status by any means. I couldn't help but wonder if my time had arrived.

As I continued to ask God for personal direction that year, nothing happened. No one called and offered me a million-dollar contract. No one knocked on my door and asked if I'd consider selling movie rights to my latest novels. No one prevailed upon me to go on a national speaking tour. Zip. Nada. Silence.

Just when I thought it couldn't get any worse, God spoke: "Somebody has to set up the chairs."

What was that supposed to mean? I played dumb as long as I could, determined to make the message go away by convincing myself it wasn't from God at all, or else that there was some wonderful, hidden meaning in the words. Neither happened. The words remained, and they meant exactly what I knew they meant.

God was calling me to a year of serving others. Oh, I know, as Christians we're all called to serve one another, and that's fine. But this was specific, and that wasn't so fine. Just when I'd thought I might expect a major breakthrough in my own work and ministry, God was telling me to dedicate myself to helping others in theirs.

I quickly found myself in yet another arm-wrestling match with God and finally gave up—2006 would be a year of service to others. What was I to do about that? How did one go about setting up a "spiritual service station" to minister to the ministers?

I thought, planned, meditated, manipulated, and even prayed, but every plan I came up with seemed doomed to fail. There are a lot of big-name ministries "out there" (I still haven't figured out where that is!), but how could I get in touch with them? By that time, even though my kids were all grown and gone with kids of their own, my mom was living with my husband and me, and I was her primary caregiver. I was also writing and editing full time, even if I wasn't getting rich or famous as a result. I was pretty much tied to working at home and limiting my trips away to a few necessary speaking engagements and/or book-signings and promotions.

My biggest problem—and the one that caused the most whining on my part—was accepting God's assignment, along with its humbling implications. Hadn't I already gone through the stages of crawling, walking, running, and flying? Now that I finally understood about resting, shouldn't the learning and serving part be behind me?

Apparently not, or God wouldn't have told me to spend the next year setting up chairs for others. Of course, even I was savvy enough to know He didn't mean that I should literally spend twelve months setting up chairs at various ministry meetings, but I was positive I was supposed to get busy and start serving whenever, wherever, and however I could.

I started making phone calls, writing letters, sending emails, and asking everyone I met how I could help them in areas of ministry. My first thought was to sign up for more activities and ministries at church, but I'd already tried that and things hadn't worked out too well. To be honest, I was a bit confused: If God was calling me to rest in Him, how was I to take on serving others without giving up my resting time?

I shared my dilemma with a couple of online prayer partners, who not only commiserated but related similar situations. We agreed to pray for each other about the dilemma, while continuing to seek God in our own lives.

Green Light

It wasn't too far into the year that a friend asked if I would consider serving as spiritual adviser to our online writers' group, since the position involved gathering and sending out prayer requests and praise reports to our members, along with a weekly devotional thought, which was something I enjoyed doing anyway. She said she thought I'd be perfect for the position, and it sounded perfect to me too.

Could this be one of the ways God wanted me to "set up chairs"? I'd be helping others in ministries much like my own—praying for them, encouraging them, sharing their challenges and victories—without having to leave home. I prayed and sensed an immediate green light, so I agreed.

It didn't take me long to realize I'd made a wise choice—one of the few in my oft impetuous life—and that was encouraging. In addition, I noticed that even though it was one more thing added to my weekly to-do list, it wasn't a burden. Every Thursday morning I spent time with the Lord, praying and reading the Scriptures, meditating and asking God for direction for the day. This was something I did every day, but Thursday became my "spiritual adviser" day, when I went straight from my time with God to my computer, where I gathered all the requests and praises that had come in during the week, put them into a group email, added the devotional thought God had given me during our time together that morning, and sent it out. It always flowed easily, and I never felt stressed by the weekly responsibility. Was it possible I was learning how to rest in God and set up chairs at the same time?

A few months later I flew to Denver to attend a conference of Christian women writers and speakers, just prior to the annual Christian booksellers' and retailers' convention. I arrived at the venue a little ahead of schedule ("punctual" is my middle name!), finding only one other member there ahead of me. It was obvious that there were a few details left to attend to before the conference could get under way—things like straightening tablecloths, checking centerpieces, and (you guessed it!) setting up chairs—so we got busy. As we chatted and worked side by side, I found myself laughing at the irony of the situation. It didn't take long for my newfound friend to join me, as I related my "somebody has to set up the chairs" marching orders for 2006. As a result, we not only set up and straightened chairs, we prayed over each one as we did. I was beginning to think this combination of resting in God and serving others at the same time was not only possible, it was the only way to minister with joy.

I was beginning to see a pattern here. Seek God, serve God, obey God, love God, rest in God—and the rest would fall into place. Matthew 6:33 was quickly becoming my motto: *"Seek first the kingdom of God and His righteousness, and all these things shall be added to you."* All what things? Peace, joy, laughter, fulfillment—and yes, rest. I marveled that I hadn't seen it sooner! Why was it that the simplest truths seemed the most difficult to grasp?

As summer turned to fall, I found myself having opportunities to "connect" people in work and ministry. In other words, a publisher or agent would be looking for a certain type of book or writer, and I didn't fit the bill but I knew someone who did. I served as a "matchmaker" and connected them. People with great stories to tell but no natural writing ability or talent to do so approached me with their need, and I knew just the person who could help write the book—another matchmaking success.

It almost seemed too good to be true. I'd become something of a clearinghouse in the writing and speaking world, and I was enjoying every minute of it. It wasn't doing much to help my own career or ministry, but it didn't seem to matter because I knew I was being obedient to set up chairs and rest in Him. I hadn't purposely orchestrated any of the things I was doing, but God was opening doors and directing me through them along the way. It was the most restful "work" I'd ever done.

Then, suddenly, another year was drawing to a close, and I found myself a bit apprehensive about seeking God's direction for the new year. Despite my previous misgivings and even resistance to "setting up chairs," I'd become comfortable and satisfied in that position, and I wasn't anxious to change.

Nevertheless, I'd learned that if I want to serve God I need to recognize and understand when the seasons are changing. I certainly didn't want to be caught in my spiritual bathing suit in the middle of a snowstorm! So I began my annual end-of-the-year pursuit of God and His direction for me. Maybe God would tell me to continue setting up chairs, and I wouldn't have to make a change after all.

I prayed and listened...and listened and prayed. I read and memorized and meditated. Finally I got two words: *submission* and *position*.

Anyone who's been in the church for any length of time, particularly if you're female, knows the sinking feeling you get when you hear that first word: *submission.* I was sure nothing good could come of it.

Yet, as 2007 began to unfold, God's purpose for the two words became clear: *Keep your heart submitted to Me, and you will be in position to receive My blessings.*

"But, Lord," I argued, "You've already blessed me so much! What more could you possibly give me?"

I couldn't see it then, but I know now that God was smiling as I asked that naive question. It wouldn't be long before He gave me the answer.

 Making It Personal

What situations or circumstances have been unexpectedly presented to you in which you had opportunity to minister to and serve others? How did you handle those situations, and what was the outcome? In addition to blessing others, how did those serendipitous ministry opportunities affect you?

Therefore humble yourselves under the mighty hand of God, that He may exalt you in due time.
—1 Peter 5:6

"UNDER THE MERCY"

If there's one thing I've learned over the years, it's that God is a God of completion. Just as He promises in Philippians 1:6, when He begins a good work, He's faithful to complete it. God began a good work in me before the foundation of the world, though I didn't become aware of it until I was born again on July 5, 1974. And He continues to carry out that good work to fulfill His purposes.

I'm still pleasantly surprised each time I become aware of God's grace at work in my life, and 2007 was no exception. As the new year progressed, the meaning of God's words to me—*submission* and *position*—began to take root in my soul. He was bringing me full circle in my desire to find a Proverbs 31 role model.

I'd like to be able to tell you that walking with the Lord for nearly 33 years had matured me to the point where I was no longer trying to pin down loose cannons as they zipped by on the rolling deck of my life—but I can't. I'm doing better at resisting the urge to control everything and everyone that crosses my path, but I still have my moments.

There was the Saturday I was scheduled to speak at the mother/daughter breakfast at church. My husband, not being a mother or a daughter, was not planning to attend and thought it would be a good day to sign up for a charity motorcycle ride where the proceeds would go to help children who'd lost parents in the Iraq war. He also invited two of his nephews, Mark and Mike, to join him. Before I knew it the arrangements had been made; the plan was that Mark and Mike would ride their bikes to our place on Friday night so the three of them could leave together early on Saturday morning.

I calculated how long it would take for me to get ready that morning, allowing enough time for my mom to get ready as well, since she lives with us and would be attending the breakfast with me, and I decided it would all work if I got up at five and everyone stuck to my predetermined schedule. There was only one problem: I thought I didn't have to be at church until nine thirty, but a couple of nights before the event I got a call from Shelly, the lady who was scheduled to open the breakfast meeting with praise and worship music.

"I'll meet you at the church at eight," she said, "and we can go over the final details then. That should give us plenty of time."

That was an understatement, since the event didn't start until ten thirty. What was she thinking? "Do you really think we'll need to be there that early? Usually an hour is plenty of time to get everything set up and do a sound check and—"

"Exactly," she agreed. "And since it starts at nine, eight should be perfect."

Where had I come up with the idea that it didn't start until ten thirty? Surely I'd read that in the bulletin, or . . .

Or not. I'd been out of town the past couple weekends, and I had no idea where the ten thirty time frame had originated. Since Shelly was there every weekend, faithfully leading worship on Sunday, I had to admit it was more likely she was right about the breakfast starting at nine—which meant I was wrong and my schedule was worthless.

I swallowed, sensing a cannonball blasting straight for my head, targeted to land right between my eyes. How in the world was I going to deflect such a deadly hit?

"No problem," I said, hoping I sounded at least somewhat confident. "I'll see you there... at eight."

When I hung up the phone I thought of a commercial that was popular a few years ago, where a guy sits at a desk loaded with ringing phones. He grabs one and says, "No problem; I can do that," then another and says, "Yes, I can do that," and then another, "Yes, yes, I'll do that." By the time he's answered all the phones and assured the callers that he'll do whatever they want done, he looks at the camera with that somebody-please-help-me look and says, "How am I going to do that?"

That was the phrase that echoed in my brain as I sat there that evening, staring at my own phone and wondering how I was going to "do that." Just how early would I have to get up to make sure everyone was ready on time? My schedule was going up in flames, and I could smell the cannon powder in my nostrils. I was going down.

I hit the floor, grabbing my Bible on the way. (At least I'd learned something over the years!) As I began to pray for direction, I sensed God reminding me of the message I planned to deliver to those mothers and daughters, which had to do with a comparison of two biblical mothers: Eve and Mary.

I turned first to Genesis and studied Eve's response to the serpent's temptation. When that conniving slimeball first slithered up to Eve he hissed, "Has God really said...?" (see 3:1). Eve replied to the attack on God's command, and then the serpent hit her with a double whammy. He not only challenged the truth of God's Word, but he also challenged the goodness of God's character:

Then the serpent said to the woman, "You will not surely die. For God knows that in the day you eat of

it your eyes will be opened, and you will be like God,
knowing good and evil." So when the woman saw that
the tree was good for food, that it was pleasant to the
eyes, and a tree desirable to make one wise, she took
of its fruit and ate. She also gave to her husband with
her, and he ate.
—Genesis 3:4–6

The serpent was telling Eve that God was holding out on her, that He didn't have her best interests at heart—all this despite the fact Eve lived in a perfect environment and she, along with her husband, had face-to-face communion with their Creator as they walked in the cool of the day. Eve swallowed Satan's lie, and the rest is history.

God Outside the Box

Then I turned to Luke 1 to reread my planned text about the Virgin Mary's response concerning God's Word and His character, which is summarized in verse 38, when she said, "Behold the maidservant of the Lord! Let it be to me according to your word."

Granted, she was speaking to the angel who'd just announced that she'd been chosen by God to bear His Son—in the natural, an impossible scenario since, as this young virgin told the angel, *"I do not know [have intimate relations with] a man"* (v. 34, amplification added). But her response was a willing submission to the message the angel had brought to her from God. Mary willingly submitted to God's Word, because she knew what He said was true—and she knew His purpose for her was right. Unlike Eve, Mary believed God's Word and trusted His character, even if she didn't understand.

What about you? God whispered to my heart. *Do you believe My Word?* Before I could answer, He continued. *If you believe My Word but continue to try to do things your way, that leaves only one conclusion: You don't trust my character. You don't truly believe that I love you and want what's best for you.*

I'd never been more devastated. I'd walked with God for more than three decades, and never once had He let me down. True to His Word (even when I wasn't), He'd never forsaken me. He'd always readily forgiven me the moment I turned to Him in repentance. He'd listened in the night when I called out to Him—even when my heart hurt too badly to speak. He'd spoken "peace" to the storms in my life and had been the Shield that deflected the loose cannons that threatened to undo me at every turn. He was the Faithful One, the Unchanging One, the Lover of my soul, the One who'd willingly gone to the Cross in my place—yet I doubted His character. I still believed I could handle at least a few of those deadly cannonballs better than He. I felt like the prophet Isaiah, who said upon seeing the majesty of God, "Woe is me, for I am undone! Because I am a man of unclean lips, and I dwell in the midst of a people of unclean lips; for my eyes have seen the King, the Lord of hosts" (Isaiah 6:5).

Oh, the mercy of God, as He wrapped me in His loving arms and allowed me to hear the beat of His great and perfect heart, a heart that we can trust because it is fully and completely good. Why had I not truly understood that sooner?

As I contemplated that question, the Lord reminded me of C.S. Lewis's *The Chronicles of Narnia*, in which Aslan, the lion who portrays our Lord in the marvelous children's stories, is described this way: "[H]e is not safe. But he is good....He's not a 'tame lion.'"

Perhaps that had been my problem all along. I had trouble believing God was truly good—all the time, regardless of circumstances or situations—because I couldn't tame Him. I couldn't put Him in a box or a cage; I couldn't predict His actions or control His behavior. So I concentrated on trying to control everyone else's—down to the hour and minute when each would take his or her designated turn in the shower so I could maintain my self-imposed schedule. Stunned, I realized I'd been treating God as if He, and not I, were the loose cannon!

As I released my pointless schedule to the Faithful One in whose arms I rested, I realized the boom of threatening cannons had faded, replaced by the strong pounding of God's heart. *This is where I need to be, isn't it? Here, listening to Your heartbeat, believing in Your Word, trusting in Your character. Oh, Lord, make me like the young virgin Mary, who had more loose cannons aimed at her than I can even imagine, and yet she trusted in Your Word and Your character.*

I was in awe, as I thought back over all those people God had brought into my life over the years to reveal to me another piece of the puzzle that formed the image of the Proverbs 31 woman. Now He had used Mary to lock the final piece into place, completing the picture that had been forming in my heart and mind for many years.

As I continued to rest and listen, I heard these words of worship, a song of rest and mercy, given to me by the God who is not tame...but who is good:

Under the mercy, all my strivings shall cease;
Under the mercy, I will rest in His peace;
Under the mercy, bringing all that I am;
Under the mercy, by the blood of the Lamb.

At last I'd found it, that place of submission, that place of rest where we receive His love and His blessings—under the mercy—not striving to "do" but resting in the Truth of His Word and in the goodness of His character.

As the loose cannons of life continue to zoom around and past us on the rolling deck of life, may we submit to that precious place of blessing, resting in Him, on our knees—under the mercy.

Making It Personal

Have you ever had that sort of "epiphany" moment when some great truth you'd struggled with for years suddenly became clear to you? How did it happen? How did you react? How has it changed your life, and the lives of those around you?

Being confident of this very thing, that He who has begun a good work in you will complete it until the day of Jesus Christ.
—Philippians 1:6

CONCLUSION

O Captain, My Captain

I've come a long way since I was six and first dreamed of becoming Superwoman. Obviously that's a dream I never fulfilled. But though I failed to fly under my own power, I learned how to rest and let God carry me wherever He wanted me to go.

When I think of my spiritual life in stages—crawling, walking, running, flying, resting—I also think of what an amazing contrast that is to "The Seven Ages of Man" by William Shakespeare, which refers to the natural life, rather than the spiritual. I was in high school and not yet a believer when I first read this poem. I remember thinking how very sad and hopeless the words made me feel, particularly the last four lines, which describe what we are left with when our earthly sojourn is over:

Last scene of all,
That ends this strange eventful history,
Is second childishness and mere oblivion,
Sans teeth, sans eyes, sans taste, sans everything.

Oblivion. Without teeth, without eyes, without taste... without everything. Sailing on a sea of hopelessness, with no one to guide or rescue us, until there is nothing left—as if we'd never existed. It's enough to reduce even Superwoman herself to a cowering mass of self-loathing.

How different when we begin the stages of our spiritual life! Though it may take awhile to realize we're not in charge—that God is at the helm and has no place for a cocaptain, if we'll stay onboard and keep our eyes fixed on Him, we'll eventually begin to rest in the fact that we're sailing on the only tight ship in the Universe. We'll also discover that despite all the loose cannons rolling around the deck, our Captain controls even the wind and the waves, and He will bring us safely home.

The Apostle Paul understood this truth well. Unlike the hopelessness of a life ending "sans everything," Paul summed up the end of his life this way:

> *For I am already being poured out as a drink offering, and the time of my departure is at hand. I have fought the good fight, I have finished the race, I have kept the faith. Finally, there is laid up for me the crown of righteousness, which the Lord, the righteous Judge, will give to me on that Day, and not to me only but also to all who have loved His appearing.*
> —2 Timothy 4:6–8

The time of my departure is at hand. Paul knew he was about to depart this earth. Though his natural body and his material possessions would be left behind to return to dust, his spirit would go on to live forever with the One who'd given him that eternal life *and* navigated him through his time on earth as well.

And so we return to my original question: How can I run a tight ship when I'm surrounded by loose cannons? I can't—and neither can you. God doesn't expect us to, because it's not our ship; it's His. All we have to do is trust our Captain, and leave the navigating to Him.

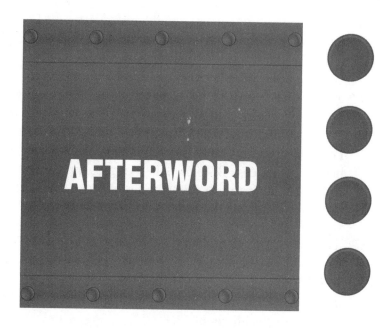

Chocolate, Coffee, and Smoking Bangs

You'd think after so many years in my crawling, walking, running, flying, resting life in Christ I would have it down so much better. But, boy, would I love a tight-ship kind of life!

Instead, I have to admit that I'm my own loose cannon. I can just picture myself holding a burning match to the cannon wick: There I stand with a gunpowder-covered face, smoking hair, and Velcro where my bangs used to be. I wish I could blame pirates for taking over my ship, but the truth is that so often I'm the only one leading the mutiny.

I feel torn between my desire to control a tight ship—on my terms—and my own loose-cannon tendencies. It's a weird blend.

While the tight ship/loose cannon blend really is a weird one, I have to tell you about another mix I've discovered. Not a weird one—a beautiful one. I recently found a new appreciation for the beauty of chocolate and coffee together. Two magnificent caffeine sources in one giant mug! I had too many the other day, and I don't think my top eyelids touched the bottom lids for about six straight hours. If tight lids meant tight ship, I would be cruising.

Yes, there have been a handful of wondrous times when my spiritual ship peacefully cruised along. How glorious! But as I catch myself holding a match to the wick of the cannon, I'm reminded how often I'm doing anything but cruising. I can convince myself that doing things my own way is what brings happiness. But in fact, trying to find direction on my own and do things my way doesn't take me in the right direction at all. It's the rudderless life. Jeremiah 10:23 says, "O Lord, I know the way of man is not in himself; It is not in man who walks to direct his own steps."

Guide my own life in the right direction? Not happening! It's just not in me. I need direction from the God of the universe. Following His direction and resting in His love— that's what it's all about.

I loved reading Kathi's account of Mara's testimony in Chapter 11. How beautifully she brings back into focus the answer to every kind of tight ship/loose cannon frustration in this life: Jesus loves me. He loves me so much more than I could ever deserve. He loves me from one side of eternity to the other with the proof of the cross right in the middle. Every tight-ship kind of battle I face is won because of His amazing love.

O Lord, may I remember your love. Thank you for loving me even when I'm overcaffeinated and underdependent, holding my mocha latte in one hand and trying to comb out my smoking, fried bangs with the other. May your love continue to remind me to rest in You every moment of every day in every situation.

May it inspire me to line up my idea of a tight ship with Yours and to completely depend on You. May my life be one constant "Aye aye, Captain!"

Father, may Your kind of tight ship become a reality for every friend praying along with me right now. All glory to you! In Jesus's name, amen.

—**Rhonda Rhea,** author of *High Heels in High Places, Purse-suit of Holiness,* and *Whatever Blings Are Lovely*

Also from *New Hope*

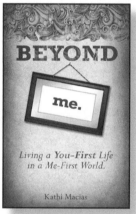

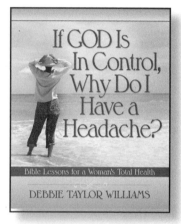

Beyond Me
*Living a You-First Life
in a Me-First World*
Kathi Macias
ISBN-10: 1-59669-220-0
ISBN-13: 978-1-59669-220-6

**If God Is in Control,
Why Do I Have a Headache?**
*Bible Lessons for a
Woman's Total Health*
Debbie Taylor Williams
ISBN-10: 1-56309-819-9
ISBN-13: 978-1-56309-819-2

**Available in
bookstores everywhere**

For information about these books or any New Hope product,
visit www.newhopepublishers.com.